BRAHMS PIANO MUSIC

BBC MUSIC GUIDES

# Brahms Piano Music

DENIS MATTHEWS

UNIVERSITY OF WASHINGTON PRESS
SEATTLE

# Contents

First published 1978 by the British Broadcasting Corporation
Copyright © Denis Matthews 1978
University of Washington Press edition first published 1978
Library of Congress Catalog Card Number 75-27955
ISBN 0-295-95480-9
Printed in England

# *Foreword*

When preparing a lecture-recital on the Brahms piano music I was asked to provide a suitably eye-catching title. The old gaffe about 'what *are* Brahms?' was far too flippant for a serious context. Yet on second thoughts it seemed to have a subtle truth lurking accidentally behind it. A programme largely devoted to the early F minor Sonata, the Handel Variations, and a group of the late Intermezzi revealed a definite plurality in Brahms's musical make-up. Was he a Classicist, a contrapuntist (his variation sets abound in contrapuntal devices), or in his heart-of-hearts a Romantic, a lyricist, dare one say a miniaturist? At any rate these differing aspects of Brahms were clearly reflected in the chronological list of the solo piano works. I finally settled on 'Brahms's Three Phases', choosing the word 'phase' in its widest sense – not only as a 'stage' but as a facet of something more enduring, just as one speaks of the phases of the moon. In brief these phases might be described as architectural, contrapuntal and lyrical. They might then be related in turn to Brahms's aspirations, his problems and his nature. There is no doubt that he felt destined to keep the Classical ideals of form alive in an age that, in general, thought them outmoded. The shadow of Beethoven hangs heavily at times over his more ambitious early works, and indeed over his long-postponed First Symphony, a point Brahms's admirers (to his supposed annoyance) were quick to observe.

At the age of twenty Brahms announced himself to Schumann, and through Schumann to the world, with three piano sonatas on the grand scale. His intense self-criticism soon led him back to Bach, who was being eagerly rediscovered even by the out-and-out Romantics of the Liszt school. Brahms was to take the lessons of the past more literally. Apart from a set of Ballades he turned to variation-form, leading up to the well-known works on themes by Handel and Paganini, sharpening his technical skill and disciplining his more daring earlier manner. He then appeared to lose interest in the piano for a while, but during the period of his great orchestral works he returned to it for groups of shorter pieces, a genre he pursued further in his last years. Some critics have felt, in fact, that the gentler and more introspective of these *Klavierstücke* represent the essential Brahms, a 'monologue' as Hanslick described them. But the three phases – or facets – of Brahms are nearly always present to some extent and, according to the forms he chose, in a different order of priority. Leaving the concert-hall after a Brahms symphony or concerto one may reflect on the overall mastery of form or the more localised skill in developing and combining ideas, but the themes themselves are likely to sing longest in the listener's memory.

Most discussions of Brahms's music gravitate back sooner or later to the first impact of the young composer on the Schumann family at Düsseldorf. The piano works make it an inevitable starting-point. Brahms was a pianist, freshly arrived from a concert-tour with the violinist Reményi, who incidentally left him with a lasting feeling for the Hungarian gipsy style that is liable to surface in his profoundest and most personal works. On their travels Brahms had shown some of his music to Liszt at Weimar, where the welcome had been somewhat dashed by Brahms falling asleep as Liszt was playing his own new B minor Sonata. The later hostility of partisans can hardly be blamed on this incident – which, fictitious or not, symbolises Brahms's notorious lack of decorum – for both Liszt and Wagner saw much to admire in the bold spirit of the early Brahms. Their paths were to lead violently apart, however, and though Brahms always recognised the genius of Wagner he did not help matters by signing a rash manifesto protesting against the claims of the so-called 'music of the future'. Both as pianist and composer Brahms had been brought up on a love of the classics, encouraged by his Hamburg teacher Eduard Marxsen, to whom he much later dedicated his B flat Concerto. He had shown some potential as a prodigy, but his talents had been deflected into the less glamorous but more immediate bread-winning appearances in taverns and dance-halls. As a composer too Brahms learnt his early experience the hard way, making arrangements of popular music and later destroying, typically, most of his more serious apprentice works.

This early background would be incomplete without mention of Joseph Joachim. Though only two years older than Brahms he had already made a reputation through his noble playing of the Beethoven Violin Concerto. Their lifelong friendship was to survive the misunderstandings that Brahms seemed unable to avoid in his personal relationships, and it was in fact Joachim who first commended him to Schumann, drawing forth Schumann's enthusiastic response: 'This is he that should come.' On his arrival at the Schumanns the twenty-year-old Brahms at once impressed his new-found friends with his playing as well as his works. Schumann's wife

6

Clara was herself a pianist renowned for her high ideals and unlikely
to be swayed by ephemeral or superficial talents. She was one of the
first to introduce the serious keyboard repertory into public con-
certs, and early in October 1853 she noted in her diary:

> It is really moving to see him sitting at the piano, with his interesting young face
> which becomes transfigured when he plays, his beautiful hands which overcome
> the greatest difficulties with perfect ease (his things are very difficult), and in
> addition these remarkable compositions.

Notice that she refers first to Brahms as a pianist. What 'remarkable
compositions' did he play on that prolonged visit to the Schumanns?
From all accounts, including Schumann's much-quoted article 'New
Paths', he offered a great deal that never survived his later judgment.
Of the 'sonatas for violin and piano, string quartets, etc.' nothing
(as far as we know) exists from that time. Brahms must certainly
have played the piano works that Schumann immediately helped
him to have published: the E flat minor Scherzo, the Sonatas in F
sharp minor and C major, and (according to Clara) his most recent
one in F minor, with which he bade his enthusiastic hosts a tem-
porary farewell. No one could have guessed that this impressive
work, still in the repertory of hundreds of pianists, would turn out
to be his permanent farewell to the form. In a further forty years and
more, largely spent in pursuing the sonata principle in the worlds of
chamber and orchestral music, Brahms never wrote – or approved –
another piano sonata.

Clara's remark, 'his things are very difficult', will not be contested
by any who have grappled with the more awkward corners of
Brahms's piano-writing of this or any period. The report that he
apparently surmounted the unwieldy climaxes of those ambitious
early works 'with perfect ease' testifies to a prodigious keyboard
command. On tour with Reményi he is said to have transposed his
part of the Beethoven C minor Sonata, Op. 30 No. 2, into C sharp
minor when faced with a piano a semitone flat. The musicianship
was one thing, the quick adaptability of fingers into a black-note
key quite another. A glance at his own F minor Sonata suggests
however that his virtuosity was of a very personal kind, fashioned
by (and in turn fashioning) the matter in hand and far removed from
conventional dexterity. The passage quoted in Ex. 1 comes at the
moment of recapitulation in the first movement, where the rhythmic
precision of the short notes is at the mercy of perilous octave leaps.
No wonder that some editions, like the Breitkopf one quoted, sug-

gested a thinning-out of the texture by omitting the notes in small type.

Ex.1

Many otherwise formidable players have been floored in such places, though they could have taken a mild consolation in accounts of Brahms's different performing problems. Years later, George Henschel discovered him feverishly practising the Schumann Concerto and the solo piano part of Beethoven's Choral Fantasy. His own strenuous D minor Concerto, he confessed, would have given him no difficulty, but by that time he found simple diatonic runs 'exasperating'.

Before attending to Brahms's piano works in more detail, it is worth recalling the musical, and musically political, situation in which Schumann's lavish praise had suddenly embroiled him: 'He comes like Minerva, fully armed from the head of Jove.' The Romantic tide was nearing its fullest flood. Before Brahms was born Berlioz had produced the *Symphonie Fantastique*, and the young Liszt (always a champion of new music) lost no time in arranging it for piano solo. Despite Berlioz's qualified title, a kind of advance warning, no traditionalist would have called the work a symphony. Schumann, while admiring its daring originality, had added that he hoped his review of it would lead Berlioz to 'moderate his eccentricities'. Even Chopin had been lightheartedly rebuked by the same pen for making a sonata (the B flat minor) out of 'four of his maddest children'. The dangers of extremism were in the air, and a rift between innovation and tradition was to become wider still with the later works of Liszt and Wagner, precipitating the critics' war in which Brahms became reluctantly involved. Elsewhere the piano, with its increased compass and newly-acquired iron frame, tempted virtuosos great and small to entertain a willing public with operatic paraphrases and fantasias, the main prerequisite being that they should sound more difficult than they really were. Lack of such superficial 'effectiveness' no doubt led to the initial downfall of Brahms's First Piano Concerto. Yet Schumann's Romanticism, as obvious in his music as in his writings, was aware of responsibility to the past. The not-so-distant past, culminating in the sonatas, quartets and symphonies of Beethoven especially, had become Classical, and the greatest works of this rich heritage had achieved a miraculous sense of proportion: craftsmanship and seeming spontaneity, with dramatic force in fact strengthened by the quest for formal perfection. Was this past still relevant to the problems of the present and the future, with the language of music rapidly changing? Schumann must have realised that his own gifts were ideally suited to a small canvas. His style remained episodic even in his most successful longer works, like the D minor Symphony, the Piano Quintet and the Piano Concerto. It is not denying the Schumann concerto its special charm to note that its recapitulations are lazily repetitious by comparison with many of Mozart's. But Brahms? It seemed clear at once that he already had a remarkable grasp of large-scale form and a complete seriousness of purpose.

Yet his early armoury, to continue Schumann's simile, contained many frankly Romantic devices seldom indulged in his later works, qualities of exuberance, rhetoric and fantasy that were so soon to fall under the glare of his self-criticism. It was Romantic to preface slow movements with poetic quotations and to make overt cross-references between one movement and another. Liszt, when Brahms visited him, must have been delighted – even flattered? – at the opening showers of octaves and the rhapsodic close of the F sharp minor Sonata. It could hardly have been foreseen that Brahms would eventually end his last symphony with a strictly-worked and soberly-scored passacaglia. Even Schumann, who only lived to know the earliest Brahms, might have been a shade disappointed – or at least surprised – at the direction his 'new paths' were to take. Yet time has proved Brahms's judgment right – for himself. Most of the old charges of conservatism have subsided as concert-bills continue to announce all of his symphonies and concertos and a fair proportion of his songs, chamber and piano music.

It was in the 1880s that Hugo Wolf, writing in the Vienna *Salonblatt*, scorned Brahms as the most worthy representative of 'the art of composing without ideas'. Wolf was not unbiased: he had shown some of his own early songs to Brahms and been told to take lessons in strict counterpoint. In an age that had just produced *The Ring* and *Parsifal*? Wolf's invective showed no mercy: 'In a single cymbal clash from a work of Liszt's there is expressed more spirit and feeling than in all Brahms's symphonies and his serenades besides.' Yet certain faint parallels exist even between the opposing schools – the increasingly contrapuntal textures of the later Wagner, and the gentle restraint and economy of some of Liszt's last piano works like *En rêve* and *Nuages gris*, so far removed from his vociferous youth. Brahms faced his conscience at a much earlier stage.

Two general remarks about Brahms must conclude this preface and both are beautifully worded. In his book *The Classical Style*, Charles Rosen ended by discussing its disintegration and its lingering influences. On the very last page he wrote that Brahms 'may be said to have made music out of his openly-expressed regret that he was born too late'. Regret was a favourite indulgence of the Romantic period and easily exploited. It colours much of Brahms's music but is more and more under intellectual control. Finally a tribute from Schoenberg, who praised Brahms's integrity and called him a progressive: 'He did not live on inherited fortune; he made one of his own.' *How* he made it is told, more than in any other single medium, by the 'three phases' of his piano music.

# Phase One – mostly Sonatas

It was natural that Brahms should take early to the piano sonata, just as it seems unnatural that he should so soon abandon it. But surely he must have written and rejected many before the 'fully-armed' three that have come down to us? Yet there is no direct evidence of any; indeed there even seems some confusion over the details of his concert appearances during his early teens. In 1848 and 1849 he gave two recitals of his own in Hamburg and at the second of them he included a Bach fugue and Beethoven's 'Waldstein' Sonata. As compensation to a public unused to such serious fare he threw in his own Fantasia 'on a favourite Waltz' with great success. Other such pieces, presumably in the popular style of the day, included a 'Souvenir de la Russie' for piano duet and were published under a pseudonym, no doubt to his later relief. Eduard Marxsen, however, mentioned 'some charming variations on a folk-theme, one of which consisted of a most successfully worked-out canon'. How prophetic on all counts! Brahms's melodic genius was constantly nourished on his love of folksong, and the association of variations with counterpoint suggests that the different elements were already at work.

The earliest of Brahms's piano works approved for publication under his own name was the Scherzo in E flat minor. Its date is generally agreed as 1851, when he was eighteen. After the meeting with Schumann there was some debate as to the order in which his works should appear. It was eventually decided to place the C major Sonata first, followed by the slightly earlier F sharp minor and then by a group of songs (including 'Liebestreu'), thus making the Scherzo 'Opus 4'.

## SCHERZO IN E FLAT MINOR, OP. 4

Brahms seemed to fight shy of scherzos in later years, though he threw in the equivalent of one where least expected – in the B flat Concerto. More often he tended to relax the resolute Beethovenish 3/4 time into 6/8 movements (the C major Trio, the F major Cello Sonata) or to turn three-in-a-bar into two (the Fourth Symphony, the D minor Violin Sonata). Possibly to avoid invidious comparisons with Beethoven he also showed a Romantic leaning to gentle moderate-paced substitutes, e.g. in the first three symphonies, in which scherzo elements might later appear (the Second Symphony, the A minor String Quartet). In his groups of piano-pieces he adopted the term 'Capriccio' as if to push the parallel completely away. But Brahms at eighteen had no such inhibitions, if inhibitions they were. The scherzos in the sonatas, which were soon to follow, all fulfil their traditional purpose in the tightening of rhythm and a closed-in form, one of the essential contrasts of the classical symphony and, when occasion arose, the four-movement sonata. Brahms's separate Scherzo might have belonged to a missing or projected sonata, though its two independent trios extend it beyond the normal time-scale. It makes a useful self-contained piece and Brahms the pianist must have found it so. The opening flourish, a four-note figure much developed, bears a superficial likeness to Chopin's in his Scherzo in B flat minor. Brahms however knew little of him at the time, and it would in any case be unkind to compare his youthful workmanship with the superb drive of the Chopin scherzos. A Beethovenish obsession with terse rhythmic patterns is more obvious, but Brahms at this stage had much to discover about Beethoven's drama of key-relations. The 'main theme' that belatedly clinches the home-key obstinately clings to it on all its appearances, remaining earth-bound with its heavy accents, and the side-slipping modulations of the rest of the scherzo proper wear thin when they come round for the third time. Of the two trio-sections the second, with a welcome and startling plunge into B major, is the more eloquent because the more song-like; but the derivation of the first trio from a figure of the scherzo itself shows Brahms already aware of problems of unity:

Ex.2

A comparison with the splendidly athletic scherzo of the F minor Sonata proves how rapidly Brahms's style was to mature within two years. Mature is the word, for the style itself – in the sense of a basic idiom or language – was to change little in a lifetime. It was to undergo subtle refinements in technique, texture and harmony. But the vocabulary remained: with Brahms there was no parallel to the vast journeys between early and late Beethoven or between *Rienzi* and *Parsifal*. Conversely, the E flat minor Scherzo is interesting for us in displaying so many typically Brahmsian traits so soon: his special use of the word *sostenuto* to denote a holding-back of the tempo, the hemiola or cross-rhythm that he could seldom resist in triple time, the orchestral solidity of the climaxes – and even, towards the end of the first trio, some mild adventures in counterpoint.

## SONATA IN F SHARP MINOR, OP. 2

It is significant that Brahms's first known sonata should have been his most extrovertly Romantic; and more so that he should have chosen the more classically-conceived C major in preference to it for his Opus 1. The F sharp minor led writers of the past into highflown prose. Richard Specht, for example, described it as 'wild and fantastic' and spoke of its 'febrile and faltering passion'. Karl Geiringer observed, with more detachment, that 'everywhere we find a romantic flow of imagination in conflict with a sense of form influenced by classic models'. The conflict was in fact on two planes, and the long-term one of form and content was to be dealt with by Brahms's self-disciplinary measures. The internal, emotional one gave some truth to Specht's remark about 'faltering passion'. Like the month of March (and Brahms's Third Symphony) the first movement enters like a lion; but it then collapses quickly into a mood of gloomy introspection. When it rallies for an impassioned second subject, Brahms's brain-work ensures that the undercurrent of triplet chords is prepared through a diminution of the dark preceding motive (Ex. 3a), and there is much to admire in the interplay of all these ideas.

If the emotions now sound rather commonplace and heart-on-sleeve – see the *espressivo* phrase quoted – this is because Brahms was shortly to learn to elevate and deepen, compress and distil such things. The dramatic return of the opening leonine octaves on an interrupted cadence, marked *furioso* in the score, is heralded by some facile bravura. In this sort of rhetoric Liszt was the master, though if he welcomed the work as from a kindred spirit he was mistaken.

The second movement is a set of variations again extravagantly laid out for its simple subject and eagerly exploiting the full range

of the keyboard. It leads directly into the scherzo, which turns out to be a further variation – another Lisztian trait ? – and after a more melodious and Schubertian trio (D major, with a grandiose climax) the *da capo* is adorned with blind-octave trills and other devices, further evidence of the young Brahms's virtuosity. The finale, a sonata-form movement with a recurring introduction and a fantastic coda, was to leave the mark of its more improvisatory moments on the cadenzas in the last two movements of the D minor Concerto.

Much has been made of the supposed likeness of the opening of the C major Sonata to that of Beethoven's 'Hammerklavier', and the sudden turn of the theme from C to B flat also had a precedent in the first movement of the 'Waldstein', which we know to have been in Brahms's early repertory. To such observations he might have replied, as he did over the finale of his First Symphony and the 'Ode to Joy', 'every fool knows that!' Brahms was wise enough himself to know that such similarities were only skin-deep. His harmonised-out first subject in the sonata, though arresting enough in itself, is a comfortably solid affair beside the titanic affirmation of a single harmony in the 'Hammerklavier' and the mysterious but far-reaching opening moves of the 'Waldstein'. Nevertheless Brahms's approach to sonata form is more assured and conscientious than in the previous melodrama of the F sharp minor just discussed. The landmarks, including exposition repeat with first-time bars, are clearly shown and prepared for. The textures too are, on the whole, sparer and more organised, with a transition leading neatly out of the first theme as though imitating a stretto of wind instruments after full orchestra. This orchestral comparison is not irrelevant, for Schumann spoke of the sonatas as 'more like disguised symphonies', prophesying the day when Brahms should 'lower his magic wand' over the larger forces. Yet in places he seemed over-eager to prove his growing craft and worth, facing the problem of choice that affected all Romantics grappling with inherited concepts of form: when and when not to 'develop', and *how* to develop. The *poco ritenuto* theme from the second group (Ex. 4 overleaf) is pure song and hardly an apt topic for argument. But at the start of the development section it is forced into an uneasy canon, and in the coda contrives to combine more smoothly with its own diminution.

How then should a composer with song in his heart but with his eye on the symphony (or the large-scale sonata) set about ordering his ideas? Song-like themes do not lend themselves naturally to dissection and development, and the marvellous motivic treatment in the Classics – especially in Haydn, Mozart and Beethoven – was seldom meted out to their *cantabile* themes unless they contained, as they often did, some rhythmic germ ripe for independent growth. The opening phrase of the Pastoral Symphony is, in this last respect, endlessly fruitful. The contrapuntal blending of ideas, however,

Ex.4

offered a different unifying prospect and proved to be the strength of Brahms's later works like the symphonies. It is not confined to canons and fugatos, and at the height of this development section in the C major Sonata Brahms seems to throw everything into the melting pot. If the result strikes one as a little forced or contrived the spirit is bold; and the same grandeur of manner characterises the splendid dominant-pedal peroration at the end of the first movement.

The Andante, like that of the F sharp minor Sonata, is in variation-form, though the piano-writing is far simpler – sight-readable for an experienced player. Its C minor theme 'after an old German *Minnelied*', i.e. love-song, is laid out as for a leading voice answered by a four-part chorus, and words are written into the score. In the variations the 'leading' phrases persist largely in the bass and there are some dallyings and digressions the later Brahms would have frowned on. At last the subdued nocturnal atmosphere is dispelled by a full-voiced C major variation, but the coda leading out of it is as tenderly Brahmsian as many dying falls in the late Intermezzi. The scherzo, in E minor and 6/8 time, is from the same stable as the earlier ones, though built out of sequences and diminutions that run through a wide range of keys. Its mood becomes stormier, and there are passages that anticipate the Beethovenish parts of the 6/8 first movement of the First Symphony, to be offset by the Romantic warmth of the trio (C major). In this latter context Ex. 3 from the previous sonata would already sound dated; and the lead-back, with the scherzo-theme ominously asserting itself, is both subtle and dramatic. In the scherzo and the finale Brahms shows his penchant for thickening pianistic octaves with thirds (or sixths), and the finale also makes much play with off-beat accents and other cross-rhythms, typical features to be better integrated in later works.

In form the finale is a straightforward rondo with some transitions and lingering farewells, especially to the second and supposedly Scottish-inspired episode. (Not that Brahms ever crossed the North Sea: but Scottish folklore attracted him, e.g. the 'Edward' Ballade, Op. 10 no. 1, and the Intermezzo, Op. 117 no. 1.) The increase of tempo in the coda, echoing Schumann's famous *noch schneller* ('still faster'), makes a climactic but conventional ending. The real weight of the sonata lies in the well-wrought argument of the first move-ment, and Brahms seemed to recognise this when he fashioned the finale's rondo-theme out of the very opening – once again a Lisztian device:

Ex.5

The balance and proportion of movements was faced more squarely – solved is too conclusive a word – when Brahms wrote his F minor Sonata close on the heels of the C major. It was to be a further remarkable leap ahead in craft and conviction, and for a contributory factor one must turn again to Schumann's comment: 'For in him resides a second genius – namely, that of modesty.'

### SONATA IN F MINOR, OP. 5

By general consent and performance statistics the F minor is *the* sonata of the three. It is certainly the one in which 'the young eagle' – Schumann's phrase again – spreads its wings with the greatest assurance. Pushing the Romantic metaphor a little further, the eagle's flight surveys a wider and more richly varied terrain than hitherto, and its newly-learned art of hovering enables features of the landscape to be observed in more detail and from different angles. In sonata terms this means that the musical ideas are more searchingly and resourcefully treated, contrasts more effectively placed, and relationships clarified. The words *fest und bestimmt*, 'firm and resolute', are written over the first movement's proud transition-theme, whose solid harmonisation is offset by a purposeful staccato figure deriving from the first subject itself (quoted obliquely in Ex. 1). The fact that this in turn yields the ingratiating second subject reflects Brahms's growing mastery of formal unity and economy:

Ex.6

All three sonatas begin in the grand manner, but the opening of the F minor casts the longest shadow over subsequent events. In the development it storms in twice, like a fierce ritornello, in keys as far away and apart as C sharp minor and G flat major. Its forceful return in the coda and in F major makes for a triumphant ending but may be felt to take the wind out of similar gestures at the end of the whole sonata. Nevertheless the youthful impulses of the early Brahms have appealed to some who have turned away from the more severe rationalism of the later (though it is hoped that none would agree with Hugo Wolf, who saw the maturer eagle as, after all, only a hedge sparrow).

The great warmth of expression in the Andante, the second movement, had been presaged in the first movement's gentler contrasts, such as the theme briefly quoted in Ex. 6 (ii). In the development, too, there had been a rapt cello-like episode in the key of D flat, subdominant of the Andante's A flat, but a subdominant to which that movement twice gravitates for long stretches – and in which, surprisingly for Brahms, it ends. The strength of key relations and associations is shown in the melodic connection between all these D flat themes, including the first-movement one, and by the fact that all three begin in a hushed mood and grow to ecstatic climaxes. An extra-musical clue is the quotation over the Andante of some lines from a love-poem by Sternau. The spaciousness of the movement owes much, however, to its opening A flat theme, a long one and completely rounded off in its ABA structure. It returns in full with a varied accompaniment and is then only hinted at in the last of the coda's several farewells, though the sonata as a whole will take a further farewell of it later. Some features of this theme may be noted: the initial falling thirds, a Brahmsian fingerprint that remained (e.g. in the Fourth Symphony, the B minor Intermezzo from Op. 119, the Four Serious Songs); a glance, subconscious perhaps, at the *adagio* of Beethoven's *Pathétique* in the rising phrase that follows (even the key and register are identical); the beautiful effect of higher register and duet-texture in the middle part of the theme; and the ideally-placed deep pedal-notes beneath the return of the first part.

Wagner heard the F minor Sonata *before* he composed *Die Meister-singer*. It would be fanciful to suggest that Hans Sachs's absorption with the 'Vogel der heut' sang' in the second act of the opera had any sly reference to Schumann's 'eagle', but Wagner's notes are strikingly reminiscent of the coda-theme of Brahms's slow movement:

Ex.7

(a) [Brahms]

(b) [Wagner]

Dem Vo - gel der heut' sang, dem war der

Schna-bel hold ge - wach - sen

Both themes, moreover, are introduced and supported by a reiterated dominant pedal, seeming to prove that even such arch-opposites (as their partisans claimed) still shared a common musical language.

After the splendidly vigorous scherzo, which starts off in a fiery waltz-rhythm but incorporates a richly-harmonised trio (again in D flat, again generating a great climax), Brahms looked back at his main Andante theme in a *Rückblick* ('retrospect'), thus giving the sonata five movements in all. Its minor-key transformation in the *Rückblick* creates an atmosphere of profound regret, even of tragedy, borne out by the starkly orchestral writing. A mysterious 'drum' motive soon breaks out in a menacing *fortissimo* and the associations with fate and Beethoven's Fifth Symphony seem unmistakable. (Beethoven's so-called 'fate' motive had loomed elsewhere in the F minor Sonata – in the first movement and the trio of the scherzo – and it was to haunt Brahms for years to come.) Eventually these two ideas fade away in the lower reaches of the keyboard and the finale follows without a break. Here Brahms qualified his marking 'allegro moderato' with 'ma rubato', inviting a freedom of execution that is already implied by other expression-marks. In fact the finale's rondo-subject, having started off in a springing six-eight time, is at once fraught with strange hesitations and dramatic outbursts of energy. The first episode, in F major, makes light of all this: its rather commonplace melodic sequences may be explained by their artificial (esoteric and Schumannesque) derivation from the notes FAE – a reference to Joachim's motto 'frei aber einsam' – with which the theme begins. The lead-back, however, is side-tracked into a quiet and fascinating development of the original rondo-theme over a pedal D flat, and the 'quasi pizzicato' added in some editions, authentic or not, is at least a tribute to the evocative texture. Episode two, yet again D flat, has a broad chordal theme that dominates the last part of the movement. Its basic nature makes it as tempting a subject for canonic treatment as 'Three blind mice' and its contrapuntal adventures and diminutions carry it with increasing excitement up to the jubilant close mentioned earlier.

So far we have been considering Brahms's piano music written up to the age of twenty. It is easy enough to criticise the piano sonatas after well over a century, even the F minor, and it is likely that Brahms would have agreed with such criticism within months of writing them. Against the poetry of the F minor's Andante, the spell-binding originality of the *Rückblick*, and the general grandeur of manner throughout, must be set some inequalities and some ungainly rampages: awkward stretches and leaps at the climaxes in pursuit of an orchestral sonority; occasional squareness of phrasing, with too many full stops in place of commas or semicolons; and a few makeshift accompanying figures, as in episode one of the finale or the discursive first-movement development. Though Brahms was to prune and discipline these traits, pianists may regret that his own reappraisal of the sonatas probably caused him to turn away from a medium he had approached so boldly. What kind of piano sonata, one wonders, might have emerged from the period of the symphonies? The two Rhapsodies, Op. 79, give us a clue, for they are far from rhapsodic in form; yet Brahms may have had reason for leading his more extended sonata-style works away from the solo piano. Colour he was to restrict more and more to musical necessity, but chamber music (and the orchestra) naturally provided a richer palette. It is worth noting that his one later keyboard sonata, the F minor for two pianos, derived from a string quintet and ended up as a piano quintet. Sets of variations, in which the challenge of contrast is both encouraged and controlled by the form itself, were another matter – but Brahms even abandoned these, as entities, when they had served their purpose for him. The first set, on a theme of Schumann, was written in 1854. So were the Ballades, Op. 10. The Variations are best discussed with the other sets that followed them, but the Ballades are too far away in time from the later piano-pieces to be linked with them.

## FOUR BALLADES, OP. 10

As a relaxation from the larger demands of the sonata – for composer and listener – the short but characterful piano-piece was a popular nineteenth-century by-product. Its history can of course be traced much further back: to the Elizabethan virginalists, to Couperin and Rameau, and (more recently) to the Bagatelles of Beethoven, the Eclogues and Dithyrambs of Tomašek, and the Impromptus of Voříšek. These last two were Bohemians working in Vienna, where Schubert's outpouring of piano sonatas did not prevent him too from writing Impromptus and Moments Musicaux, many of them long-beloved of amateur pianists. The variety of labels increased, many of them disarmingly non-committal as with Mendelssohn's *Songs without Words*. Schumann, however, was more liable to group his miniatures under some more specific programmatic heading, for example, *Carnaval* or *Kinderszenen*, and their musical unity was clarified by – even at times dependent upon? – their picturesque subtitles. His *Phantasiestücke*, whether subtitled or not, were more independent pieces, closer in spirit and intention to the Brahms Ballades, which may or may not be played as a set. And what does the term 'Ballade' imply? A musical parallel to a narrative poem, hence a piece of 'programme music'? Or a fairly free but uncommitted work, dramatic in character but still 'absolute music' like the Chopin Ballades?

Brahms's first Ballade is unique among his instrumental works in following an extra-musical programme, that of the grim Scottish ballad 'Edward', which he knew in German from Herder's *Stimmen der Völker* and later set as a duet for alto and tenor (Op. 75 no. 1). The story of Edward's patricide, revealed in a mother-son conversation, is dramatically evoked in Brahms's piano 'setting', with the great climax built up to the accompaniment of the Beethoven 'fate' rhythm already noticed in the F minor Sonata. In the end the bleak opening theme is heard against a broken-triplet figure, with a chilling effect that Brahms, had he chosen, might have taken into the world of opera. The other Ballades have no such overt impulse, though the second and third have strongly contrasted middle sections (as does Brahms's very much later Ballade in G minor, Op. 118, no. 3). The second (D major) has a wide-spanned theme of the type most perfectly fulfilled in the song 'Feldeinsamkeit', and the initial notes FAF – admittedly F sharps – were possibly Brahms's response 'frei aber froh' to Joachim's FAE motto mentioned before – and more famously responded to in the Third Symphony. No. 3 in B minor is the scherzo of the set (Capriccio?) though it is curiously labelled Intermezzo. In 6/8 time it has a predictable play with cross-rhythms, but the unpredictable half-close at the end of the first part sets off a middle section in quiet root-position harmony and high registration that affects, and subdues, the return in this otherwise simple ternary piece. The fourth of the Ballades is at a glance the most Schumannesque; but the economy of the writing, the emotional restraint, with inner voices 'senza troppo marcare' (hinted at rather than brought out), and the play with five-bar phrasing, all betoken Brahms's later manner.

Meanwhile Clara Schumann played a Gavotte and Sarabande by Brahms that, like much of his music, never ascended into print. Remarks from her diary of 1854 record the prevailing tastes, tensions and prejudices: on 13 May Brahms's wonderful playing of Schubert's B flat Sonata, with reservations about his 'exaggerated' tempi; on 25 May a friendly letter from Liszt 'enclosing a sonata dedicated to Robert' (the B minor) which Brahms played to her. 'Nothing but noise . . .and to crown all I must write and thank him – it is really dreadful.'

## Phase Two – entirely Variations

Within five months of Brahms's introduction to the Schumann family, Schumann's mental health broke down. His attempted suicide was described in a letter from Albert Dietrich to Joachim (28 February 1854):

In a recent letter to Brahms I hinted that Schumann's nerves were in a bad state. This has become worse from day to day; he heard music continuously, sometimes of the most beautiful kind, but often agonisingly hideous. Later on, phantom voices were added to this . . .

Dietrich was another of the circle of composer-friends, with whom Schumann and Brahms had collaborated in a surprise 'FAE' violin-and-piano sonata for Joachim. (Brahms's contribution, a scherzo in C minor with a very Beethovenish opening and a lyrical Schumannesque trio, was published posthumously as a 'Sonatensatz'.) The remaining two and a half years of Schumann's life, mostly spent in the asylum at Endenich, cannot be detailed here, though a letter from him to Brahms, undispatched and for long unknown, must be quoted at length. It amounts to a rapturous appreciation of a work Brahms had sent him.

## SCHUMANN VARIATIONS, OP. 9

That you have studied counterpoint deeply is apparent in all the Variations. How tender, how original in its masterly expression, how ingenious every one of them! How I should like to hear you or Clara play them! And then, the wonderful variety! The 3rd, the 4th, the 5th, the 6th with its retrogression in the 2nd part. The following Andante, how tender; the 8th with its beautiful second part. Then the 9th, how beautiful in form; the 10th, how full of art, how tender; how individual and delicate the 11th, and how ingeniously the 12th joins it! Then the 13th, with its sweet metaphysical tones, and next the Andante, with its witty and artistic canon in seconds, and the 15th in G flat major, the 16th beautifully and blessedly in F sharp major.

Schumann never sent these lines but substituted a more toned-down letter of thanks. The theme of his in question was the first 'Albumblatt' from a mixed group of pieces called *Bunte Blätter*, Op. 99. Brahms worked on the variations during the summer of 1854. The crisis had drawn him still closer into the family circle and the further title, 'Little Variations on a Theme of His, dedicated to Her', shows the degree of intimacy. To strengthen the dedication further Brahms included a subtle reference to a theme of *hers*, as he explained to Joachim (12 September): 'My Variations have had two new additions, in one of which *Clara speaks*!' The variation was the tenth – 'how full of art, how tender' – and Clara's theme, quoted as an inner voice in bars 30–1, had already been the subject of Schumann's own Impromptus, Op. 5. To keep the work even more 'within the family' Brahms's previous variation had adopted and adapted Schumann's *second* 'Albumblatt' from Op. 99.

These personal gestures, like the Joachim-Brahms FAE-FAF exchanges, were all in line with the Romantic climate of Schumann's *Carnaval* and they can scarcely affect the ultimate value of a work of art to the uninitiated. Some other variations seem more outward tributes to Schumann's style: the left-hand staccato of no. 2, per-haps, to the first of the *Études Symphoniques*, and the expressive arpeggios of no. 15 to the A flat section in the Piano Concerto. But Schumann's unposted letter had mentioned counterpoint first of all. The ingenious inversions, e.g. in the bass of Clara's variation, and closely-woven canons – especially in no. 14, quoted in Ex. 8 – were an outcome of Brahms's continuing studies, smoother and less self-advertising than the contrapuntal escapades of the sonatas.

Ex.8

Variation form demanded more, of course: a fidelity to the structure and phrasing of the text, though not disallowing a gradual harmonic expansion. It required the punctual carrying-through of a figuration or texture, the fulfilment of each variation's character with a further eye on the work's overall shape. The degree of liberty permitted was a matter for the composer's own conscience, and in this Schumann set Brahms made some extensions and compressions more freely than in, say, the later Handel and Paganini ones. This was in keeping with Schumann's own more Romantic view of the form. Or was it that Brahms's Classical conscience had not yet been fully alerted?

The theme, in F sharp minor, is tenderly wistful, and the final 'blessed' variation resolves its yearnings with a *ppp diminuendo* in the tonic major. Yet it is also a firmly-shaped theme in its clear four-bar phrasing, and Brahms always chose such themes as a starting-point. In their different ways the exotically irregular Hungarian Song of Op. 21 no 2 and the five-bar phrases of the 'St Antoni' chorale are equally clear-cut. Schumann's reharmonisation of his first four bars on their return (bars 17–20) had an uncanny precedent in the slow movement of Beethoven's C minor Sonata for violin and piano (bars 20–2), the work Brahms had been obliged to transpose up a semitone when on tour with Reményi. Since Schumann was moving to A major, and Beethoven's theme was in A flat, Brahms's fingers must have felt 'we have been here before':

Ex.9

  (a) [Schumann]

  (b) [Beethoven]

The variations Op. 21 nos. 1 and 2 can hardly be considered a pair, and the shared form seems the only excuse for the sharing of an opus number, the common key of D major being a better one for keeping them apart – from the programme-maker's point of view. The first set, on an original theme, is of interest for the important step it takes towards the stricter form about which Brahms wrote to Joachim, not to be confused with the far easier-to-write fantasias which often masqueraded as true variations. Brahms's own theme, however, lacks the clear sense of direction of his other variation texts. Its warm-hearted opening phrase over a tonic pedal is beautifully shaped, but yields to more workmanlike sequences and, in the second half, to a frustrated climax. The sequences avoid squareness by bringing a five-bar reply, dutifully noted in all the variations, but one feature of the opening is never exploited and (disappointingly) never returns – the delightful turn-of-phrase in bars 3 and 4, to be recalled in the first minuet of the orchestral Serenade in the same key. The year was 1856 and the restraint and caution of the writing led to many 'pattern' variations devoted to a single figure or textural device, including more fiery ones like nos. 8 and 9. In no. 8 (D minor) Brahms hit upon a keyboard pattern – dotted-rhythm chords filled in by staccato left-hand leaps – that was to be the essence of the last of the Handel Variations and the solo climaxes in the first movement of the B flat Concerto. The idea of pairing or grouping variations was traditional: nos. 8 and 9 are, in character, such a pair, and at the start the pure pattern of no. 1 provided a flowing accompaniment to the melodic no. 2. In the fifth variation Brahms the contrapuntist is at work again with an involved canon in contrary motion, presenting the player with two main problems: how to negotiate the ingenious but sprawling left-hand part 'teneramente' as marked; and whether to read the inverted canon in twos or threes, a relic of the ambiguities (to us) of Baroque notation (Ex. 10 overleaf). The set ends with an extended finale, and the gradual build-up over left-hand trills invites comparison with the variations in Beethoven's Op. 109 Sonata. If the expected comparable climax is diverted into a further page of mundane afterthoughts, this is perhaps in line with the unsensational though affectionate enough nature of the original theme.

Op. 21 no. 2 is concerned with a Hungarian theme, and although the gipsy element continued to attract him, the topic and style

Ex.10 Var. 5

**Tempo di tema**

*molto e dolce*

*molto espressivo*

*p* *teneramente*

*legato*

*Canone in moto contrario*

*sempre col Ped.*

suggest that Brahms might have conceived the work at an earlier date, probably during the Reményi tour of 1853. He was to make a Hungarian style very much his own in the finale of the G minor Piano Quartet, thereafter absorbing this element into his natural musical speech. In the variations the theme is of paramount importance since its harmonisation is primitive. Indeed we never move far away from it, and its thundering reappearance at the end is a popular gesture remote from the intimacies of the previous set or the Schumann Variations. The Hungarian Song's regular alternations of 3/4 and 4/4 bars are followed by Brahms in eight variations, the first six of them in the minor key. But by no. 9 the rhythmic pattern palls and is abandoned; and in the final wind-up, leading out of no. 13, a simpler two-plus-two phrasing is jostled into and out of three-plus-two (compare the five-bar reply of Op. 21 no. 1) until the theme itself settles the argument.

## HANDEL VARIATIONS, OP. 24

From 1856 onwards the name 'Herr Brahms, J., Tonkünstler' appeared in the annual list of subscribers to the Bach Gesellschaft edition, and in that year the work published was the Mass in B minor. This systematic reassessment and revelation of Bach was a great compensating factor in the Romantic period, and though the purist may frown on the rage for pianistic transcriptions of his organ works by Liszt, Tausig and others, they had historical, indeed pioneer, value. Bach's influence on Brahms ran deeper into his own style. He too made a few transcriptions but more of pedagogic than public interest. His arrangement of Bach's violin Chaconne for left hand alone is understandably less known than Busoni's full-blown two-hand one; and another solo violin piece, the final presto from the G minor Sonata, was arranged by Brahms in two versions, giving Bach's original to right and left hands in turn. Other adaptations included Weber's C major Rondo, also a largely left-hand exercise, and a more simple and affectionate one of a Gluck gavotte. But one 'after Chopin' doubled the delicate melodic line of the F minor Study, Op. 25 no. 2, with nightmarish thirds and sixths, an experiment best confined to the practice-room – which was probably Brahms's intention anyway.

Meanwhile Brahms's D minor Piano Concerto, his first large-scale orchestral work, had brought in the soloist with a quiet and Bach-like theme that turned such thirds and sixths to its own purpose. The fiasco of its Leipzig performance (27 January 1859) was described to Clara with remarkable detachment: 'My concerto went very well. I had two rehearsals. You know already that it was a complete failure.' The public and the players had been unprepared for such unadorned seriousness and profundity, to which the tragedy of Schumann's death contributed; and though the work was later recognised as a masterpiece Brahms wrote no more orchestral music, apart from completing his two Serenades, until the 'St Antoni' Variations of 1873. The solo piano works helped to make these possible, and in 1861 Brahms applied himself to an Air in B flat by Handel, which had already been used by Handel himself as the subject for a short set of harpsichord variations. The theme was ideally suited to Brahms's severer approach, in style and structure, and its melodic line is given in Ex. 11:

Ex.11

Handel's theme made an admirably neutral starting-place, with none of the subjective overtones that characterised Brahms's previous variation subjects. (Even the rowdy Hungarian Song of Op. 21 no. 2 was exotic and had its Reményi associations.) In choosing Handel for his largest set of variations Brahms looked back beyond the Classical period to the Baroque. The ornaments in the theme demand a crisp harpsichord-like articulation, a precision that is carried over into the first variation, a 'pattern' one that throws off brilliant up-and-down scales at the cadences. But the Handel tune also has a ceremonial character typical of its period: indeed it is not unlike the popular Jeremiah Clarke 'Trumpet Voluntary' that used to be ascribed to Purcell, and in his orchestration of the Brahms variations Edmund Rubbra actually gave the opening to a trumpet. Rubbra's was a worthwhile experiment (1938) since a well-conducted orchestra can give pianists many lessons in accentuation and phrasing, as for example in the usually misheard because misplayed no. 3 – which too easily sounds 'on the wrong foot' – and in the stressed-and-held mid-bar chords of no. 25. Yet as with Weingartner and the 'Hammerklavier', and purism apart, attempts to score Brahms's more massive variations end by leading one back to the self-sufficiency of the original. This does not absolve the Brahms player from the need to think orchestrally in order to draw the strongest contrasts from a mere keyboard. Variation 6 inevitably suggests muted strings, and no. 7 a trio of horns, to the present writer, and to imitate a trumpet in the theme is far better than to render it tentatively or colourlessly.

The theme has important features beyond its basic harmony and binary form. There is a firm accompanying rhythm in the regular pattern

♩ ♩ ♩ ⁷ ♪ | ♩ ♩ ♩ ⁷ ♪ | ♩

and with equal regularity a right-hand semiquaver figure that soon acquires the significance of a 'motive'. It is to become the mainspring of the final fugue. The experienced variation-writer would naturally seize upon such details, and the reproduction of bar 1 a third higher in bar 3 gave Brahms opportunities for modulating sequences, replacing the theme's tonic harmony with the third-higher mediant or, in a minor variation, the relative major. The half-close in bar 4, the full close in bar 8 and the rising progression of bar 6 were also landmarks – or theme-marks – doubly noted on account of the repeats. Binary themes with repeated halves had long been favoured as variation texts, since the composer's concentrated art could also be heard twice (unless he chose to vary it himself in a 'double variation'). Beethoven's Diabelli Variations had thrived on a more extended though in itself less dignified theme of this type, and Tovey obviously had the Diabelli and Bach's 'Goldberg' in mind when he ranked the Brahms-Handel with 'the half-dozen greatest sets of variations ever written'. Although it would take the most avid Brahmsian to place his in the exalted company of two such towering masterworks, when it comes to a half-dozen it would be hard not to agree with Tovey. Brahms's craftsmanship and resource are not in doubt. He had neither the power to approach, nor the wish to imitate, the cosmic range, daring imagination, and spiritual heights of late Beethoven. If his emotions and his textures are less awe-inspiring they are for many listeners more comforting and accessible. A few later sets of piano variations may go down to history for an originality Brahms never aimed at – Webern or Copland perhaps – though none, to one's knowledge, embracing the wide humanity of Bach or Beethoven. The Brahms-Handel nevertheless retain a reputation and, in the best sense of the word, a popularity above all rivals of their period.

It would have been easier for Brahms to have sought extra variety by key-changes. Beethoven rode round a whole circle of keys and time-signatures in a delightful set of variations, Op. 34; yet on the much vaster scale of the Diabelli he rejected such methods, relying instead on sheer musical invention. He turned only once to the tonic minor in his first twenty-eight variations, then settling in the minor for a group of three, plunging dramatically into a fugue in the relative major, and returning to the home-key (C major) for a final ethereal transformation of Diabelli's waltz. These last events are shattering because the lengthy period of key-stability had almost ruled out their possibility. In the Handel Variations Brahms accepted the stability, calling on the tonic minor three times (in nos. 5, 6 and 13) and the relative minor once (no. 21) but making no such startling long-delayed disclosures. His final three variations are cumulative, building up a great climax in no. 25, and the fugue sails in with the absolute assurance that despite its darker episodes it will carry Handel's original B flat to an even more exultant conclusion.

The order of the variations in a large set presents problems and invites arbitrary decisions. On a smaller scale the simple effect of cumulation may suffice, as in the middle movement of Beethoven's 'Appassionata' Sonata, where quicker note-values and rising pitch produce a logical climax. Such a process could scarcely be extended to twenty-five variations lasting as many minutes, and contrasts require careful planning to ensure a feeling of progress and to avoid a piecemeal effect. Brahms's first four Handel variations are strongly contrasted, and though the smooth triplets of no. 2 lead gracefully into the quaver appoggiaturas of no. 3 these are brushed aside by the stormy octaves of no. 4. Nos. 2 to 4 have already indulged in minor-key inflections (try playing D *flat* in bar 5 of the theme), a Brahmsian habit that might be thought a musical manifestation of Rosen's remark about his 'openly-expressed regret'. All this prepares the way for nos. 5 and 6, a pair of variations *in* the tonic minor, the former the most lyrical (and regretful?) so far, with an undulating melodic line that is treated in quiet octaves and strict canon in no. 6. As if this were not enough, part two of no. 6 *inverts* the right-hand canon effortlessly:

Ex.12

The pairing of variations continues in B flat major with nos. 7 and 8, brilliantly rhythmic, and nos. 11 and 12, tenderly melodic. Meanwhile the intervening ones call for the keenest 'orchestral sense' from the pianist, no. 9 with chromatic lines emerging from held pedal-notes (which die away too soon in the upper register), and no. 10 with energetic exchanges as though between groups of wind and strings. No. 9 had read D *major* harmony into bars 3 and 4, and varied its second repeat by lifting a whole phrase up a semitone from F to F sharp (alias G flat, as the following variation explains). The danger of such moves lies in the arousal of expectancy and risk of disappointment, for nothing as startlingly dramatic occurs again. Textures absorbed Brahms more, and the rich sonority of no. 13, with its suggestion of off-beat muffled drums, makes it, emotionally as well as statistically, the centrepiece of the set.

To Tovey this minor-key *largamente* conjured up a 'kind of Hungarian funeral march'. With the gipsy style went the fiddler's thirds and sixths with which Brahms loved to double a melodic line. (We meet them in the finale of the B flat Piano Concerto, second subject; more expectedly in the Violin Concerto, written for Joachim; and even in an introspective song like 'Immer leiser'.) The opening of no. 13 would just be playable with its sixths in the lowest reaches of a viola, and the cadential flourishes all contain the augmented interval G flat–A natural, adding to the gipsy flavour. In variation 14 sixths of a more virtuoso kind break in, setting off a chain of five variations in which ideas are passed on from one to the next: no. 16, for example, is rather like a flute-and-bassoon caricature of the trumpet-and-drums no. 15. By no. 18 the bustle has subsided, and nos. 19 to 22 are all quiet variations not noticeably interrelated. No. 15, incidentally, had added one extra bar to the structure, an exception that proved the rule; and the low-lying chromatics of no. 20 are a splendid case of daring and discipline going hand in hand. In part two the harmonic inflections lead perilously far afield, but Brahms brings them back home with absolute smoothness and punctuality:

Ex.13

The preceding variation, no. 19, is in a 12/8 *siciliano* rhythm. Its marking 'leggiero e vivace' removes it in character from the gently beguiling one in the 'St Antoni' set, though they share a Brahmsian tendency to hide the melodic line in an inner part. So does no. 21 (in G minor) where the main notes of the theme are merely graced in passing, giving it a lightness of texture that no. 22 carries over naturally with a musical-box effect over a drone bass – a tribute to the musette of the Baroque era? This lighter mood comes late in the day, but if we look for contrast as well as unity in a set of variations, contrast is immediately provided – as Tovey put it, 'swarming up energetically out of darkness'.

In the exciting approach to the final fugue one would ask that pianists maintain a firm and constant rhythm during variations 23 to 25, instead of rushing at no. 23 like a bull at a gate and leaving no room for the subdivisions of no. 24, which is once again a variation-on-a-variation. The fugue also called for some vigorous rhythmic impulse to carry it through, and Brahms derived its subject from the opening of Handel's theme by introducing the all-pervading upbeat figure, which ties up so well with the semiquavers in the theme itself:

Ex.14  Fuga

The whole is more redolent of one of Bach's great organ fugues than of any in 'The 48',[1] with inversions, augmentations and double counterpoint to match, and a great peroration over a swinging dominant pedal-point. It proclaims the increasing skill and allegiance of a composer still in his late twenties.

Clara Schumann lost no time in learning the Handel Variations, but a note in her diary reveals the perverse side of Brahms's nature:

On Dec 7th [1861] I gave another soirée, at which I played Johannes' Handel-Variations. I was in agonies of nervousness, but I played them well all the same, and they were much applauded. Johannes, however, hurt me very much by his indifference. He declared that he could no longer bear to hear the variations, it was altogether dreadful to him to listen to anything of his own and to have to sit by and do nothing. Although I can well understand this feeling I cannot help finding it hard when one has devoted all one's powers to a work, and the composer himself has not a kind word for it. . . .

Brahms was certainly strange. He made no mention to his friends, though eye-witnesses vouch for it, that Wagner of all people praised the variations for showing 'what may still be done with the old forms, provided that someone appears who knows how to treat them'. An amusing and human anecdote was recorded by George Henschel and has a close bearing on the allegiances of the final fugue. When he and Brahms were being entertained at Koblenz by a certain Councillor Wegeler, a rare bottle of Rauenthaler was produced and sampled. Their host likened its excellence among wines to Brahms's among composers, whereupon Brahms immediately called for 'a bottle of Bach'.

---

[1] Except perhaps for the A Minor in Book 1, which is very organ-like in character and with which Brahms's fugue has affinities.

The living legend of Paganini's violin-playing was to find a near-parallel in the pianistic exploits of the young Liszt. But Paganini's twenty-fourth Caprice has had a lasting fascination for composers of very different climates: Liszt, Schumann, Brahms, Rachmaninov, Blacher, Lutoslawski. Of course the theme makes a suitably basic variation text and as such Paganini had used it himself. It also has associations with virtuosity, in fact devilish virtuosity, and in Rachmaninov's popular *Rhapsody* the quotations of the 'Dies irae' seem to follow naturally in its wake. Brahms called his variations 'studies' and published them in two sets of fourteen, the fourteenth in each case developing into an extended finale. This has not stopped some pianists from picking and choosing and others from playing both sets at one sitting, a habit Peter Latham has called 'tiresome'. Tiresome and tiring, one might add, for the Brahms Paganini Studies differ from most nineteenth-century virtuoso works in that many of them are far more difficult than they sound to the average listener. Just as the fugue of the Handel Variations was devoted to solid musical thought with no room for flamboyance or easy effect, the Paganini sets really amount to the codifying of a piano style and technique directed to similar ends.

It says much for Brahms's new discipline that his Studies should also have been, in the strictest sense, variations. In this context his expected use of double counterpoint and inversions served an extra purpose, that of sharing muscular as well as musical problems between the hands. A pair of quotations from nos. 1 and 2 of the first set illustrates this—Ex. 15 opposite. The exchanges are not slavishly exact, any more than many of Bach's, but the right-hand octave doublings also have value as studies. Octave displacements, or shifts, were another essential part of Brahms's pianistic armoury, demanding the player's ability to make quick lateral movements rather than abnormal stretches. One seldom finds, even in the wilder excursions of the earlier Brahms, unarpeggiated chords beyond the octave, and the more exacting passages in his concertos depend as much on marksmanship as graspsmanship. Variations 3 to 5 of the first Paganini set bear this out. No one's grasp could take in the quaver arpeggios of no. 4, and the 5151 fingering is the only answer, notwithstanding the leaps between 1 and 5 and vice versa —see Ex. 16, p. 38.

In variation 5, too, octave shifts continually exercise the left hand

in its crossing of the right with a chromatically 'displaced' counter-point. The threes-against-twos of the crossings hint at a 6/8 rhythm that comes out undisguised in nos. 6 to 8, a family group of varia-tions, and hangs over in the accompaniment of no. 9. But here

Ex.16

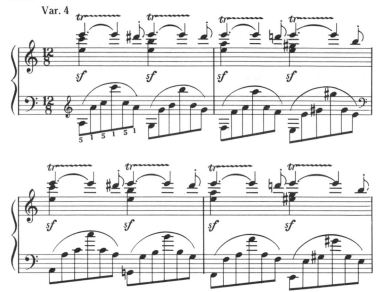

alternative harmonies crowd on to the scene, alerting the eyes and ears of the analytical sleuth. Closer inspection will confirm that full justice has been done to the structure of Paganini's theme: to its self-repeating first part, despite Brahms's varied cadences; and to the descending sequences of part two, which close in as diminutions towards the end. These and other points are far too numerous to quote in music-type, but a glance at the score will make them clear.

Adherence to the plan of the theme inhibited Brahms's melodic vein when he turned to the major key in variation 11, which he sought to alleviate by stressing the left-hand doubling in the tenor register. He gave himself a freer rein in the delightfully decorative sequel, also in A major. The original spirit of Paganini returns with the minor key: in no. 13 with the panache of its octave *glissandi*; and no. 14, which bandies the main figure of the original theme between the hands until more Brahmsian patterns herald the coda–which generously throws in a complete extra variation of its own. Before embarking on the second set one might reflect on the 'devilish' quality of Paganini's A minor theme that the normally sober-minded Brahms took to so readily. Had he, and had Paganini for that matter, memories of Beethoven's fieriest piece of violin-writing in the *Kreutzer*, also in A minor – and devilish enough to spur on one of Tolstoy's short-story characters to a crime of passion?

Brahms's second book, after restating the theme, launches into a double variation, i.e. with varied repeats, thereby compressing the value of two studies into one. The hands take turns with scale-passages in thirds and eventually combine by pulling them octaves apart, with an exciting effect like organ registration. The modulations are also exciting without masking the general structure. It might be argued that such manoeuvres presuppose a knowledge of the previous set. But that is the composer's affair, and Brahms in any case pulls himself up, adopting simpler harmonies and textures for a while. No. 4 in A major is a waltz to be played 'con grazia', and sounds a misfit if sentimentalised: its childlike sequences are saved from banality by the interestingly wide spacing between the hands. Is it a 'study'? In texture and pedalling perhaps – and also in taste. The waltz-rhythm continues as virtuoso elements creep back with the minor key, and no. 6's triplet arpeggios with grace-notes are violinistic as they stand, except for some too low bass-notes in the second part. Pianists who have trouble with threes-against-fours will find a real teaser, but a genuine study, in no. 7:

Ex.17

Var. 7

Here the rhythmic problem is further complicated by the sub-division of the threes into triplet semiquavers phrased across the beat; but the effect is winning when it comes off, particularly when (as we expect) the hands interchange. This was presumably on Clara Schumann's list of 'witch variations'. Variation 8 is once again pure Paganini, with its imitation of stratospheric harmonics and alternating pizzicato, reflected in contrary motion by the left hand. (A variant – printed in small type and therefore second-best? – crowds in more harmony at the expense of the general character.) Nos. 8 to 11 produce an internal symmetry of their own, the middle two calling for masculine weight, the outer ones lightness and agility. The extraordinary harmonic effect of no. 10 derives from long-held appoggiaturas that send off rockets of arpeggios in their own right. In no. 11, balancing no. 8 in lightness, 'blind octaves', the technique of intermingling real octaves and single notes, are exploited, creating a scintillating effect enhanced by some piquant harmonic inflections in the second part, parodying the previous variation's at the same point.

It is worth comparing Brahms's very different approaches to the finales of the two sets. In book one he started variation 14 vigorously, piling climax upon climax and only dropping down in volume to pick up his 'extra' variation, then building up again gradually through the last page. On the other hand the second finale is in reality one long crescendo, plans having been laid as far back as variation 12, the only one in either set to establish a foreign key, F major. Such a change at such a stage was often a feature of Beethoven's codas, giving freshness and drama to the home-key's return; and on the much larger scale of the Diabelli Variations he delayed the plunge until the penultimate fugue. Brahms's move was a gentle one, and no. 12 is the most Romantically melodic in the set with its broad 6/8 time yielding typically to a feeling of 3/4 in alternate bars. Its mood influences no. 13, which turns back reluctantly to A minor, breaking impulsively into a more full-voiced song of regret on the repeat of its second part. The 'motive' here is a downward scale with augmented intervals poignantly stressed, e.g. D sharp for D natural, and the same idea is taken up briskly and playfully in no. 14. As before, the actual finale develops from the end of this but encompasses *three* more cumulative variations with the minimum of extraneous rhetoric.

The Paganini Studies were composed in 1862 and 1863 and published in 1866. Thereafter Brahms appeared to give the solo piano a long rest and he never returned to it for variations. Two other sets of keyboard variations, one for piano-duet and the other for two pianos, must be mentioned in relation to what we have called his 'second phase', but the different media demand a separate chapter.

# Duets for One and Two Pianos

Works for four hands at one keyboard were very rare indeed before the time of Mozart. A five-octave compass gave little scope for manoeuvre to two adults seated side by side, though this problem hardly concerned the nine-year-old Mozart and his sister on their visit to London. However, his early C major Sonata, K.19d (written in London), was to be followed by four later ones. Two of them were mature masterpieces which established the medium as a serious contribution to chamber music. Schubert, with a wider keyboard at his disposal, was even more prolific and might be considered the patron saint of four-hand duettists. Beethoven wrote far fewer original duets, but accepted the form as a useful substitute to the extent of arranging his string quartet 'Grosse Fuge' for it. For economic and domestic reasons the earlier repertory, whether of true duets or of transcriptions, far exceeded that for two pianos. Brahms attended to both genres, though both his two-piano works also appeared in other versions, and he made or approved duet and two-piano arrangements of his orchestral music as a matter of course. During Schumann's illness he undoubtedly consoled Clara by playing duets of various kinds with her, including Robert's *Bilder aus Osten* (a set of six Impromptus) and an arrangement of his orchestral Overture, Scherzo and Finale. Clara complained that it was not easy to play with Brahms: 'he plays too arbitrarily and cares nothing about a crotchet more or less'. At that same time the ailing Schumann wrote down a beautifully tranquil theme that he believed to have been given him by the departed spirits of Schubert and Mendelssohn. This 'letzte Gedanke' was to be the subject of Brahms's one substantial four-hand duet.

## SCHUMANN VARIATIONS, OP. 23

On 1 July 1862 Clara Schumann wrote to Joachim, excitedly quoting the opening bars of the first movement of a symphony Brahms had sent her (it was the C minor but minus its introduction and uncompleted for a further fourteen years). She added, 'You know his variations for four hands on Robert's last theme, don't you? They too are admirable.' A final note referred to their enjoyment, in duet form, of Schubert's D minor Quartet, C major Quintet, and Octet. The Schumann Variations, not to be confused with the Op. 9 ones, were composed in the same year as the Handel set (1861) but were obviously designed for a more intimate audience, if for an audience at all. The first variation has decorative semiquavers in the treble – 'primo' and 'secondo' are invidious terms for genuine duet-writing – but they lead to richer and more sonorous textures in nos. 2 and 3. No. 4 in E flat minor, however, has the character of a threnody with its bleak octaves and quiet drum-like effects. Its significance is more fully understood at the magical enharmonic turn to B major for the next one, in a gently lilting 9/8 and with a consoling theme in Brahmsian thirds and sixths taken in turn by the two players. The order of the next four variations seems more casual, though the faintly Hungarian flavour of no. 8 (G minor) obviously had its 'meaning'. But everything is summed up in the final march of no. 10, triumphantly in E flat major despite its solemnly funereal dotted rhythm, and the work then fades away with lingering memories of the original theme.

It is not belittling the work to suggest that its best moments are the quietly reflective ones, for Brahms needed the more conventional vigour of variations like nos. 6 and 9 to set them in relief. By the highest standards of four-hand writing, that is to say of Mozart and Schubert, Brahms's fuller textures call out for the orchestra that at the time he avoided facing. Yet his choice of medium was in a personal and Schumannesque way appropriate to his topic. The piano duet even had its therapeutic value when intimate emotions were involved, as Edward Speyer recalled in his memoirs, *My Life and Friends*. Speyer was an ardent music-lover whose long life (1839–1934) brought him into touch with generations of famous names. He was once taken by Brahms to a private meeting of Clara Schumann's pupils:

They were apparently under the impression that they were called together to hear Brahms play. But Brahms refused, and there ensued the usual dispute between him and Clara Schumann as to which of the two was to play. After this had lasted some time, they compromised by playing the beautiful four-hand variations of Brahms on a theme by Schumann in E flat. . . . The morning I am speaking of was a cold grey day in January. Suddenly, however, a ray of sunshine shone through the windows and illuminated the venerable and noble heads of the two great artists. A deeply touching and unforgettable sight.

## WALTZES AND HUNGARIAN DANCES

No survey of Brahms's piano music would be complete without a brief mention of these popular pieces that made his name a household word even in more lowbrow circles. The Waltzes, Op. 39, and especially no. 15, became so hackneyed in arrangements that it is often forgotten that they started as four-hand duets. Brahms's move to Vienna brought him into close touch with the music of the Strauss family, and he once quoted the main theme of 'The Blue Danube' in a musical autograph with the words 'unfortunately *not* by Johannes Brahms'. He did not, and could not, enter into direct competition but he brought his serious North German craft to the waltz-rhythm and relied on the simplest of binary forms. The influence worked in reverse too, as in the near-waltz second subject in the first movement of the Second Symphony. The most direct ancestor was Schubert, whose piano music Brahms continued to play with pleasure and who had grouped together sets of dances in a similar way. Brahms's two books of *Liebeslieder* waltzes have a stronger Viennese flavour, but duettists who have played or heard them with a vocal quartet will find a non-vocal performance colourless. The four sets of Hungarian Dances, in which Reményi accused him of poaching, are also original four-hand music. So were Dvořák's Slavonic Dances. In each case the immense popularity of some of the dances led them far beyond the domestic enjoyment of amateur pianists. Dvořák orchestrated all his own and some of Brahms's too.

## SONATA IN F MINOR, OP. 34B

The material of Brahms's only two-piano sonata is identical with that of the Piano Quintet, Op. 34, but the subtitle 'after the quintet' refers to its still earlier form as a string quintet with two cellos. The two-piano version therefore represents a middle stage in Brahms's search for the ideal medium, and in this form Brahms played it in Vienna with Carl Tausig in 1864. Clara Schumann was away in Russia on a concert tour and had some misgivings about Brahms's successful collaboration with a virtuoso of the opposite camp. Brahms had had his own doubts about the string-quintet version, and the weight of two keyboards gave greater strength and solidity while preserving the conversational effect of antiphony. Yet the richness of strings was now missed, and whole sections of the sonata were criticised not for their musical content but for having the air of an orchestral transcription. There was loss in the string-conceived slow movement, in the gently ruminating part of the first-movement coda, and the similar *poco sostenuto* introduction to the finale:

Ex.18    Finale
**Poco sostenuto**

Even in the final version the solitary pianist will sometimes find his left hand deputising for a missing second cello, e.g. in bars 3 to 5 of the lowest stave in Ex. 18. The Piano Quintet on the whole offers the best of both worlds and in this form the music is analysed in some detail by Ivor Keys in the BBC Music Guide to the Brahms Chamber Music. The two-piano version is, however, important as an authentic and large-scale addition to a limited repertory of classics. Its homogeneous texture may even be felt advantageous to a study of the work's essential architecture.

Private performances of orchestral works in duet arrangements were common enough, and indeed valuable in giving a foretaste of some forthcoming première – but the case of the 'St Antoni' Variations differs from the inevitable two-piano adaptations of the symphonies. As with his Op. 34 Quintet, Brahms signified the equality of the two versions by labelling them Op. 56a and b. The familiar title 'Haydn Variations' is now generally discredited, since Haydn (according to expert sources) had borrowed a traditional theme himself in the wind Partita from which Brahms learnt it. Again Brahms had chosen a clear-cut variation subject, and the five-bar phrasing of its first strain gave him added scope. The technical polish and strict control of detail are outstanding, but it was now 1873 and ten years after the last variations, the Paganini Studies.

Counterpoint now runs more smoothly than ever, whichever version we choose, though it takes a good pianist to match the legato octaves of first and second violins, violas and cellos, in the first variation – see piano 1 in Ex. 19 overleaf. The double counterpoint here (the even quavers were at first above, the triplets below) is firmly held in place by the repeated B flats in piano 2, and these with striking economy clearly refer to the close of the 'St Antoni' chorale itself. In variation 2 (B flat minor) the first piano keeps to the wind-parts and the second to the strings of the orchestral version. There is no attempt here or elsewhere at interchanging for the sake of doing so, thus lessening the danger of outright competition that is nonetheless the spice of many two-piano works. In no. 3, which has its own antiphonies in part two, the decorative element is largely assigned to the second piano. The fourth variation is a contrapuntal *tour de force* in which the repeat of each section inverts the flowing semiquaver accompaniment in double counterpoint at the twelfth, a notoriously difficult procedure. The art conceals art, and the effect of dignified pathos does not depend on academic analysis. The rapid 6/8 scherzo of no. 5, however, stands or falls on the agility of the players just as it does on the split-second timing of strings and wind. Its lightness of touch takes in cross-accents and hemiolas, the latter emphasised by their translation into pianistic 'blind octaves'. Even players ignorant of the orchestral version would surely respond to the complementary nature of nos. 6 and 7, the former demanding the biting precision of a wind-band, to be followed by the mainly string colour (and tenderness) of a *siciliano*.

Brahms scored the mysteriously scurrying no. 8 for muted strings and pianissimo wind, including piccolo and contrabassoon. In the two-piano version he extended the sprawl of the arpeggios and omitted some points made in Op. 56a: string trills reflected by clarinets and piccolo in part one, with a cadence in G flat; and an inner melody in oboe and horn at the end of part two. These could easily have been integrated and they leave little doubt that the two-piano form predated the orchestral one. No. 8, in either case, remains remarkable for its contrapuntal ingenuity.

In the finale too, far from flying free, Brahms continued the variation discipline over a five-bar ground bass derived from the theme. On its ninth statement the first piano has a melodic line spread in broad but rhythmically awkward minim-triplets over each bar. Few will deny that the more straightforward orchestral version is also more natural and elegant, and it is offered to pianists as an alternative. Eventually the ground bass takes over the melodic line itself in the minor key, and the grand resumption of the 'St Antoni' theme in its undeniable B flat major is thereby enhanced. Without this finale, would the passacaglia of the Fourth Symphony have been written? It is fascinating to observe how the period of piano variations ended by leading Brahms back to the orchestra from which he had fought shy for so long. The two versions of the 'St Antoni' Variations bridged the gap and provided the entrance, and the larger orchestral works soon followed. As far as the piano itself was concerned, Brahms could relax a little. His 'second phase' had served its purpose and left its legacy.

## *Phase Three — Shorter Piano-pieces*

The grander schemes and larger unities of the early piano sonatas and the period of variations had now been channelled away. The orchestra absorbed Brahms, and within five years the 'St Antoni' Variations had been triumphantly followed by the first two symphonies and the Violin Concerto. In the year of the concerto, 1878, he signified a more intimate approach to the keyboard by completing the eight *Klavierstücke*, Op. 76. The title, literally 'piano-pieces', is the genre of all his remaining solo works, including the two more robust Rhapsodies of Op. 79, which are 'pieces' in the

Ex.19

sense of being independent and self-contained. The favourite sub-titles became, according to character, 'Intermezzo' or 'Capriccio' – the former on the whole more gentle and ruminating, the latter more fiery and vigorous.

Some of these pieces may have been written earlier (but which?), and their neat publication in two books, each containing two Capricci and two Intermezzi, seems more a matter of commercial convenience than artistic deliberation. Brahms's close friendship with Elisabet and Heinrich von Herzogenberg yielded a valuable exchange of letters about his music, and in November 1878 Elisabet wrote begging for copies of some 'longed-for Intermezzi' that he had played them on a visit that September. She was by all accounts as musical as she was charming, and set her plea to a theme from the Intermezzo, Op. 76 no. 7, cleverly (if not quite accurately) remembered. Her memory was, however, sensitive enough for us to take her addition of a *stringendo* and *rall.* in the latter part of the quotation as evidence of the freedom of Brahms's playing. The theme in question is given (in the published notation) in Ex. 20:

Ex.20

Brahms sent some of the pieces, still in manuscript, and Elisabet handed them over to a 'slow-coach' Leipzig copyist – except for the B minor Capriccio (no. 2) with which she would not part. This was copied 'on the spot' by a young English music student who was also reported as having composed 'the prettiest gavottes and sarabandes': her name was Ethel Smyth.

The unsuspecting purchaser who acquired the first four of Brahms's Op. 76 on the strength of the playful charm of the Capriccio just mentioned might register surprise, if not alarm, on finding its namesake, no. 1, a gloomy stormscape. There seemed a certain irony in Brahms's use of the word Capriccio, literally 'caprice', to cover turbulent or pessimistic emotions, and it can hardly be by chance that six out of his seven examples in the piano music should be in minor keys. (Yet how on the other hand could he have called the passionate outburst of Op. 118 no. 1 and the high drama and pathos of no. 6 in that set 'Intermezzi'? Perhaps the labels were after all irrelevant, or themselves capricious, when the characters were so clear.) Schumann might have called this first F sharp minor piece a 'Nachtstück', and Clara spoke of it as 'horribly difficult'. Much of the technical difficulty lies in the smouldering opening figure (Ex. 21), which soon flares up in a menacing crescendo, continuing to tax the right hand even when a peaceful close in the major key is reached.

Ex.21

The main contrast, of manner rather than mood, comes with a yearning cantabile theme, more passionate than consoling. It takes a despairing view of the four-note motive that Mozart treated so exultantly in the finale of the 'Jupiter' Symphony, and recalls the pianistic texture noted in the last of Brahms's Op. 10 Ballades. In relation to his 'second phase' it is significant that Brahms treats this idea in augmentation and inversion. At the return of Ex. 21, too, he interchanges the left- and right-hand material in Paganini-variation fashion.

The favourite B minor Capriccio (no. 2) is, however, entirely light-hearted in spite of its minor key, like the popular F minor *Moment Musical* of Schubert with which it has some superficial affinities – in the simple left-hand accompaniment and the quick contrast of the relative major. In this piece, wrote Peter Latham, 'the gypsies make their one and only appearance in the piano solos', but they are a well-groomed and orderly company. Brahms's variation-art dresses up the returns of the theme in different disguises, and its continuing staccato beneath the mock-passionate middle section demands a player's skill to match the composer's. Here the high B flats that find their way home enharmonically as A sharps were the subject of another of Elisabet von Herzogenberg's postscripts, referring to the eloquence of Brahms's playing and his 'way of making the notes sing on all sorts of pianos'. The coda fades away with a similar blend of humour, delicacy and harmonic finesse.

Two Intermezzi follow, both of them described by Clara Schumann as 'little pearls' (nos. 3 and 4). Despite the reservations about labels these pieces establish a pattern to be followed by many of the later Intermezzi: a tender mood, deepened perhaps but not disturbed by a middle section. Yet there is the difference of individuals, for whereas no. 3 in A flat takes a simple ternary form ABA with a closing reference to B, no. 4 in B flat is really a miniature sonata-form movement. It has a well-defined cadence-theme in thirds and sixths, heard first in G minor but later in the tonic; and a development hovering over, though never actually settling in, the remote region of C flat major. At a glance the delicate texture of Op. 76 no. 4, with its internal tied notes, recalls the Couperin of *Les Baricades Mistérieuses*. This is hardly accidental, for Brahms knew Couperin's keyboard music well through his collaboration in Chrysander's edition. Clara did not quite share his enthusiasm for it: 'I have often been amazed, and was so again today, that he can so delight in the old masters before Bach. . . .'

The second 'book' of Op. 76 sandwiches two more Intermezzi between two more Capricci. In the C sharp minor Capriccio Op. 76 no. 5, another agitated one, the right and left hands keep up a 3/4 versus 6/8 controversy for eighteen bars, at which point the left hand quietly drums out the 3/4 rhythm. These conflicting pulses then lead in alternation to a fierce climax that restores the opening. But Brahms's rhythmic experiments lead further in this case (they completely confused Clara Schumann) and a 2/4 time breaks in, bringing its own variation of the first theme. The start of the coda, in which the held right-hand notes give the gist of the theme, is quoted for its extreme of complexity:

Ex.22       *cresc. e string.*

The A major Intermezzo (no. 6) makes a far gentler play with threes against twos. It opens with a rocking figure in which harmony is content only to hint at melody in a Bach-like way, but it soon yields a more vocal melodic line. The 'trio' in F sharp minor is wholly melodic. It may be compared with the corresponding section in Op. 118 no. 2, a later Intermezzo in the same key and with a similar mood-contrast. No. 7 in A minor is the one quoted by Elisabet von Herzogenberg. The fragment given in Ex. 20 is expanded into a binary theme with repeats, the expression depending on first-beat dissonances and suspensions. The whole is framed by a more austere introduction and coda, with something of the bleakness of the opening of the 'Edward' Ballade, Op. 10 no. 1, though by comparison quite restrained and undramatic. Brahms was hesitant about including the final Capriccio in C major in the group: curiously, for it is an exuberant and effective piece with a thrilling climax and a touching moment of repose before the end. Once mastered, it is gratefully brilliant to play – yet perhaps for these very reasons the cautious Brahms felt it, at first, too extrovert for its context.

These later Capricci, Op. 76 nos. 5 and 8, emphasise a trait mentioned in passing at the start of this survey (in the E flat minor Scherzo): Brahms's obsession with the hemiola, briefly represented by the equation

$$\text{♩.} \quad \text{♩.} \quad = \quad \text{♩} \quad \text{♩} \quad \text{♩}$$

This cross-rhythm of three beats in the time of two, or vice versa, was a time-honoured device familiar enough in Renaissance and Baroque music; and the rhythmic ambiguities in the finale of the Schumann Piano Concerto have brought sweat to the brow of many conductors and pianists (doubtless including Brahms himself, who was found practising it 'feverishly'). With Brahms the temptation to cross 3/4 with 6/8 or 3/2 became a mannerism that lost some of its desired effect through over-indulgence. Hardly a waltz from the delightful *Liebeslieder* escaped, and even Brahms's cadenza to Mozart's C minor Piano Concerto switched to a 6/8 rhythm at the climax, as if parodying his own style. In the song 'Von ewiger Liebe' too, he disrupted the accompaniment at the closing words about enduring love – was this a touch of cynicism or simply a trick of craftsmanship he could not resist? It seems fair to conclude that Brahms's genius was more melodic and harmonic than rhythmic in the short-term sense. He was not destined to inherit the tremendous dramatic force and resource of Beethoven's rhythms, though the hammer-blows of the Fifth Symphony resounded in many of his earlier works and indeed in the C minor of his own First Symphony. A more personal hallmark was the springing iambic pattern so familiar in his orchestral masterpieces, breaking out at identical places in the lyrical first movements of the Second Symphony, the Violin Concerto and the B flat Piano Concerto, and giving added vitality to the close of the exposition.

After the intimacies of most of the preceding set these two pieces strike a grander manner, as though orchestral sonorities (understandably enough) had temporarily echoed in Brahms's keyboard style. He dedicated the two Rhapsodies to Elisabet von Herzogenberg and originally called them 'Capriccio (presto agitato)' and 'Molto passionato'. Note again the minor-key associations: the first is in B minor, the second in G minor. For their publication in 1880 he suggested their present title, and Elisabet's reply would appear to reflect Brahms's own mind on the subject:

As to your inquiry, you know I am always most partial to the non-committal word, *Klavierstücke*, just because it is non-committal; but probably that won't do, in which case the name *Rhapsodien* is the best, I expect, although the clearly defined form of both pieces seems somewhat at variance with one's conception of a rhapsody. . . . Welcome then, ye (to me) nameless ones, in your nebulous garb of rhapsodies!

The dictionary definition of a rhapsody as 'an emotional irregular piece of music', akin to a written-down improvisation, will certainly not fit in either case. Emotion there is in plenty (both are stormily passionate), but the form is firmly under control. The first has a complete 'da capo' and coda, and the second all the outward manifestations of sonata form. Yet neither could have been taken or mistaken as actual sonata movements, according to Brahms's usual tenets. Both start off in a mood of development rather than exposition, with restless sequences that in themselves could inspire the epithet 'rhapsodic'.

The Rhapsody in B minor, Op. 79 no. 1, in fact proceeds at once to treat its arresting opening phrase to some abrupt modulations and hand-to-hand exchanges in a free double counterpoint before coming to a firmly prepared cadence in the dominant minor:

Ex.23

**Agitato**

This cadence-idea with its exciting rising octaves and staggered descent is to be dramatically extended later on, and the whole process is of course reheard on the 'da capo'. Had Brahms as usual been practising Bach? It was a dozen years since the BGA had provided him with its volume of the keyboard concertos. A short quotation from the first movement of the most-played Bach D minor suggests a 'descent' of a more genealogical kind:

Ex.24

A feature of the Rhapsody admired by Elisabet was the arrival early in the first part of a D minor theme with all the appearance of a 'second subject', interrupted, however, by a lengthier and stormier development of the opening material. It was left for this hinted-at theme to fulfil itself in glorious tranquillity as the middle section or 'trio' in B *major*. This is a musette with an intriguing five-bar phrasing that varies as the drone-bass changes in pitch, pressing for modulations. The diatonic tune eventually hovers between major and minor thirds in a Schubertian way, thus making for an easy and logical resumption of the opening. Can we bear to go through that initial series of dramatic events a second time without change? Brahms apparently thought so, but he avoided a mechanical symmetry by adding a coda in which the original version of the musette-theme appears gloomily in the bass. Even the B major ending is hardly a relief, with low-lying C naturals threatening it until the last two bars of all. (Perhaps Brahms's special connotation of 'Capriccio', on an enlarged scale, was not so far from the mark.) A note on performance: it is as well that the original 'presto agitato' was replaced by 'agitato' alone, since the character of the piece requires the clear articulation of the semiquaver triplets in the first bar. These become as much a 'motive' as those in the opening subject of Beethoven's F minor Sonata Op. 2 no. 1. A steadier tempo will assist and not reduce the effect of agitation, which relies on such details and loses in a commonplace headlong rush: it will enable the B major 'trio' to float in without any violent change of gear – and Brahms indicated no such change.

A famous drawing of Brahms by Willy von Beckerath shows the composer enjoying the end of a cigar and playing the piano with his left hand reaching across his right. The work being played might have been the Rhapsody in G minor, in which musical and not acrobatic reasons dictated the hand-crossings in the first subject, enabling the right hand to sustain the internal harmonic support. (A similar passage occurs in the second movement of the B flat Concerto, from bar 67 and other places, and for similar reasons.) Such sonorities, aided by well-placed sustained notes, were typical of Brahms's piano writing and always carefully calculated. In the case of the Rhapsody the effect is rich, which only the prejudiced, and careless performers, could render as 'muddy'. (Yet complaints of muddiness used to be levelled at Brahms's scoring too. One of the greatest virtues of Toscanini's conducting of the symphonies was clarity, which depended on a scrupulous regard for the balance of the inner parts and for Brahms's own markings.) 'First subject' for the G minor Rhapsody is the right label, for sonata form is here carried through precisely. The typical iambic rhythm soon appears in a kind of transition theme, though the iambics are in the triplet rhythm that has prevailed from the start. Whether the dotted quavers and semiquavers in the march-like second subject should fit in with or differ from the triplets is a moot interpretative point. Was Brahms again adopting earlier notational conventions? But the augmentation of this theme in the development, and his love of twos (or fours) against threes, support the reverse view.

The second subject's internal and external triplets, oscillating on a dominant pedal (at first in D minor), have a somewhat oppressive effect like that noted in the early E flat minor Scherzo. A deliberate contrast to the aspiring first theme? Yet as the development progresses this too is kept harmonically in check by the triplets, until the moment of recapitulation allows it to fly free like a bird from a cage. There is a fatalistic feeling about the G minor Rhapsody that separates it in character from the previous B minor one, though that also has its share of turbulence. No human voice arises from the depths to alleviate the close of the G minor: all that is allowed is a brief extension of the final cadence, cut short with an abrupt Beethovenish gesture. Thomas Hardy, had he been a composer, might have written the G minor but scarcely the B minor Rhapsody, one reason why they are performable as a contrasted pair despite occasional similarities.

Brahms published no more solo piano music for a further dozen years. Pianists can hardly complain, for in 1881 he completed the B flat Piano Concerto, which he described with typical humour as 'a tiny, tiny piano concerto with a tiny, tiny wisp of a scherzo'. The scherzo, physically taxing for the soloist, enlarged the scope of a work already on a large scale, and the whole of the unusual four-movement scheme presents one of the most exacting but rewarding challenges in the repertory. Meanwhile Brahms tabulated his thoughts on piano technique, particularly relevant to his own style, in a series of fifty-one exercises (*Uebungen*) published by Simrock in 1893. They are not offered as works of art like Chopin's Studies but exploit a variety of keyboard patterns and problems in a didactic way. At the start they encourage five-finger exercises in the closest chromatic position, gradually extending the hand into the formulas that abound in his works, with special attention given to notes held on by specific fingers. The fifty-first and last exercise suggests a way of mastering the blind-octave variation in the second book of Paganini Studies. Yet how much was Brahms a virtuoso in the accepted sense? In his early days his technique was, according to Clara Schumann, phenomenal – if technique is regarded as a means to an end. He could hardly have conceived (and performed) the solo parts of either of his piano concertos without a 'magisterial command'. In later years he had a composer's justifiable excuse for finding less time and less real need to practise. Richard Specht, a famous biographer of Brahms, only knew him in the last decade of his life but made comments on his playing that add much to an understanding of his last sets of piano-pieces. Many of them Specht claimed to have heard fresh from the manuscript 'in the intimacy of his room'. Let him continue:

Each time – and each time in a different way – he made an indelible impression upon me. He had by then given up all concert-giving and therefore all regular practice. His technique was equal to any difficulty encountered in his own works, but it was not dazzling; he would often play as if to himself and was then capable of muttering the choicest things into his beard and failing to draw the least attention to them. His touch was sometimes hard when he played loudly, but in delicate passages magically fragrant, songful and rich in light and shade. It is certain that I have never heard anyone else play Brahms's piano music as the creator played it himself . . . the whole man was in the performance.

Before embarking on these final manifestations of Brahms's 'third phase' a brief *Rückblick* or retrospect is called for. After the two Rhapsodies of Op. 79 the orchestral world continued to absorb him. The B flat Concerto was preceded by the Tragic and Academic Festival overtures and followed by the last two symphonies and the Double Concerto for violin and cello. From the piano another long silence: except of course for its part in the concerto and its continued role in chamber music and songs.

Six years after the Fourth Symphony, and four after the Double Concerto (his last orchestral work), Brahms turned again to the solo piano. It may not have been as revealing and soul-searching a return as Beethoven's to the string quartet after the labours of the Ninth Symphony and the *Missa Solemnis*, though it had the similar significance of a withdrawal from a public to a private world. It revealed the inner depths of Brahms's mind and character, as he relaxed from his symphonic achievements into the intimate and essentially Romantic composer many believe to have been the 'true' Brahms. This does not lessen one's admiration for his hard-won triumphs in the larger Classical forms. The symphonies stand on their merits and, as Schoenberg implied, they have no direct rivals. They live on their own fortune – and so in their reverse way do the concentrated miniatures of the late Brahms piano-pieces.

It is sometimes argued that this fortune, great though it turned out to be, was earned through over-cautious investment. It could even be held against Brahms that in his large-scale works he tended to put all his material through the same mill, the same process of cerebral development, an aftermath of the disciplinary period of the piano variations. One could hardly visualise Beethoven, for example, making a fugue out of the lyrical second subject of the first movement of the Fifth Symphony. Yet no theme of

Brahms, however song-like, was entirely fugue-proof, not even the warm opening subject of the Second Symphony or that of the slow movement of the Fourth. His intellectual obsession with cross-rhythms has been dealt with and will recur again. He would have been the first to admit that he had neither the daring nor the daring simplicity of Beethoven. It was well said that he would rather construct a bridge than risk leaping over a chasm, but he was a superb constructor of bridges. One direct comparison will make this point more strongly. The finales of Beethoven's G major and Brahms's B flat piano concertos both end with a coda in quicker time. On the verge of his coda Beethoven seems to allow the soloist complete freedom, maintaining unity through an unobtrusive pizzicato falling fifth, and this simple feature of the rondo-theme is all that is needed to set the new tempo going. Brahms is more cautious and more workmanlike: he puts logic before drama, smoothing over the join with a variation full of ingenious subdivisions.

This revelling in craftsmanship was inseparable from Brahms's nature and his music, though of the B flat Concerto Hugo Wolf had to have his usual say: 'Whoever can swallow this piano concerto with relish may look forward with equanimity to a famine.' It would have been interesting indeed to have seen this and other works of Brahms in the making, but although he obviously made sketches he was systematic in destroying them along with his many unapproved compositions. A few changes of thought are referred to in his correspondence with the Herzogenbergs, with Clara Schumann and Joachim; and one radical revision is preserved in the two widely-separated versions of the B major Trio Op. 8, dating from 1854 and 1891. His ideals remained the earlier masters and, apart from Bach, the Viennese Classics. Of the slow movement of Haydn's Symphony no. 88 in G he said that he would have liked his own ninth symphony to sound like it. Some advice on composition that he gave to George Henschel could have come from Beethoven:

Let it rest, let it rest, and keep going back to it and working at it, over and over again, until it is a complete, finished work of art, until there is not a note too much or too little, not a bar you could improve on. Whether it is beautiful also is an entirely different matter, but perfect it *must* be.

The collective title of these seven pieces is curious, since the mixture of Intermezzi and Capricci is the same as with the *Klavierstücke* of Op. 76. It may have had an esoteric purpose, since 'fantasy' was a favourite term of Schumann's and Brahms had been currently involved in the preparation of a new Schumann edition. In November 1892 he agreed to help Clara over a volume of 'posthumous' works, and simultaneously he sent her eleven new pieces of his own which she described as 'full of poetry, passion, sentiment, emotion'. It was fifty-four years since Schumann himself had written to her about his *Kinderszenen*, a collection of thirty or so miniatures (from which he eventually selected twelve, then adding a postlude, 'The Poet speaks'). They were not children's pieces but pieces *about* children, with picturesque titles recalling events and emotions from the distance of maturity. Clara had been warned to forget that she was a 'virtuoso'. Brahms's late pieces of course indulged in no programme and are far from childlike, but the nostalgic quality of the Intermezzi especially aroused Clara's own memories, turning her mind back with renewed enthusiasm to Schumann's much earlier groups of pieces.

In Op. 116, however, the Capricci retain their minor-key fire, as if making a deliberate effort to throw the Intermezzi into sharp relief. The shade of Paganini hangs over the first, in D minor. Needless to say that in an energetic 3/8 *presto* there soon appear sequences of hemiolas, but the opening itself (octaves and repeated notes) is phrased across the bar lines, engendering a syncopated rhythm in which the third beats carry most of the stresses and the main harmonic changes. A further important idea, quoted in Ex. 25, shifts the accent back to the second quaver of the bar.

Ex.25

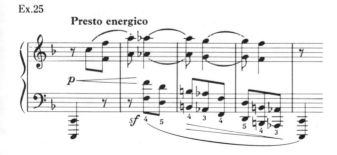

These frequent changes of step, with the hemiola pattern creeping upwards between whiles in chromatic chords, make this an exciting piece from many angles – rhythm, dynamics, texture and tonality. A particularly Brahmsian effect occurs when the first theme appears in skeletal chords *pianissimo* and in C sharp minor. Yet the strange character of the Capriccio cannot be accounted for in such objective analysis. It is dramatic but spare in material, mercurial yet ghostly, with flashes of virtuosity kept in check by intellectual absorption or turned aside into shadows – until the climactic last page. Shadows of a more vivid kind crowd into the final cadence as canons between the hands reach up the keyboard, a device Brahms could now afford to throw away almost as an afterthought. In short, it is still a 'private' piece in spite of its athleticism. It reflects rather than displays a virtuoso manner, and in so doing accords with Richard Specht's ear-witness account of the later Brahms: 'He always played as if he were alone; he forgot his public entirely.'

The second of Op. 116, an Intermezzo in A minor, brings back the truly introspective Brahms: a gentle *andante*, almost a sarabande, with quietly echoed cadences and the minimum of decoration. Within its scale it also represents a form Brahms made particularly his own, a slowish movement incorporating a scherzo-like episode or episodes. The single episode or 'trio' here is in gently shimmering broken octaves to which the left hand adds delicate chromatic inflections, and its 3/8 time is to be carefully measured against the crotchets of the first part, in which a triplet accompaniment prevailed. The sectional double-bars do not break the continuity; nor can the piece really be said to modulate – except, on the return, to the tonic major and then not for long enough to demand a change of key-signature. A printed alternative for the middle part takes the shimmer out of the right-hand octaves in order to clarify the upper melodic line, but is hardly preferable.

Op. 116, like Op. 76, was published in two 'sets' – in this case groups of three and four. Again one questions the significance of the order of the pieces, for they remain individuals with little sign of the 'sonata' sequence that Schumann detected, for example, in the characters and the key-scheme of Schubert's second set of Impromptus. 'Set one' of Op. 116 admittedly makes a symmetry out of its two Capricci and mid-placed Intermezzo. But 'set two' – with three Intermezzi (E major, E minor, E major) ruthlessly crushed by a final ferocious Capriccio in D minor? Here there seems a good excuse for picking and choosing, as most pianists do and Brahms probably did. Yet, reverting to the first set, the passions of the G minor Capriccio (no. 3) seem less convincing because they are by now over-familiar, having been more cogently expressed in the Op. 79 Rhapsodies. The slight changes in the *da capo* of the Capriccio look and sound like rather desperate attempts to avoid monotony. Played on its own the piece is effective enough in a belated 'Sturm und Drang' manner, and it has a comfortably conventional contrast in the heroic style of its middle section (E flat), which recalls the much younger Brahms of the sonatas. But there is none of the strange originality of its symmetrical partner, the first in the series.

Both the E major Intermezzi, nos. 4 and 6, owe their initial moods to tender use of the chromatic passing-note B sharp leading to C sharp. As an expressive device this progression through the sharpened dominant, usually in an inner voice, had Romantic associations with longing and nostalgia – not to mention its mildly Tristanesque connections. It was a special feature of nineteenth-century Russian music, for example Borodin and Rimsky-Korsakov, but for this Brahms showed little interest. Nor did his honest respect for Wagner make him succumb to the explicit chromaticism of *Tristan*. (It may have been the fear of succumbing that made him tell Henschel: 'If I look at *that* in the morning I am cross for the rest of the day.') Such chromatics, however, had long been part of the language of tonality – think of Mozart! – and Brahms was no more immune from their potency than Wagner. More reserved, certainly: the opening of Op. 116 no. 4 is a left-handed gesture and the consoling replies are at the start wholly diatonic—see Ex. 26 overleaf (note that the right hand crosses over the left in order to give added depth). When the chromatic B sharps assert themselves more strongly later in the piece they are either deflected into appropiate keys or gently subdued. For all its longings this Intermezzo is an answer to the minor-key ones of Op. 116 no. 2 (A minor), and a richly sweeping theme with harp-like accompaniment completes the idyll of emotions recollected in tranquillity.

The next Intermezzo, in E minor, has at first sight a purely intellectual interest with its questing dissonances mirrored between the hands. Its offbeat chords and onbeat single notes led Alan Rawsthorne to compare it to its detriment with the lilting second theme in Chopin's A flat Ballade. There is, however, no valid com-

Ex.26

parison: Brahms did not aim here at charm or ease, and there may have been a deliberate irony in his indication 'con grazia ed intimissimo sentimento'. Intimate sentiments are not always idyllic – a knowledge of Brahms's life and outward character would bear this out – but the middle section and coda resolve the tensions with a warmth of heart that goes beyond mere compositional needs and philosophical detachment.

No. 6, in E major again, poses no such internal problems: it is a favourite Intermezzo, and the B sharp passing-notes, now in an inner voice, add immense distinction to its opening theme. But where does the true melody lie? As a hard-won contrapuntist Brahms thought automatically in terms of double counterpoint even when he chose not to advertise it. Such informal surroundings hardly called for a display of learning, and the veiled conversational quality does not belie the music's nature as a 'monologue'. The middle section in G sharp minor, with its underlying hemiolas, only hints as it progresses at its potential as a tenor and soprano (or alto?) duet – another tranquil recollection?

A final Capriccio in D minor dispels all such intimate thoughts. It seems an offshoot from the larger-scale Brahms, reliving (rather than recollecting) the turbulent emotions of the C minor First Symphony and making much play with a brusque figure based on diminished-seventh harmony – an essential ingredient to be used, in

Beethoven's words, 'with discretion'. This Capriccio is surely in-
discreet, for the opening gestures lead to nothing more significant
than a 'trio' that indulges a staggered cross-rhythm effect to the
bewilderment of player and listener alike. A departure from the
straight ternary form is provided in a *crescendo* link derived from the
first idea, a device (Rawsthorne would have agreed) that Chopin
would have used with far greater subtlety. At the end Brahms
recalls his 'Paganini' manner and closes up his diminished sevenths
into chords in 3/8 time. A set (or sets) of piano-pieces may demand
contrasts in mood and pace; but it is in the Intermezzi of Op. 116
that the essence of the 'late' Brahms resides, and this label he applied
exclusively to the next group of pieces.

## THREE INTERMEZZI, OP. 117

When Schnabel took the Op. 117 Intermezzi to show to his teacher
Leschetizsky, his own enthusiasm was damped by expressions of
surprise amounting to dismay. In an age of high pianistic virtuosity
how was it possible to follow one unspectacular *andante* with
another and, on turning the page further, with a third? These
three Intermezzi, the first two especially popular, are therefore
seldom played as a group, but the experiment is profitable. Each
has its dark moods and internal contrasts, but there is adequate
variety of texture and treatment between them. The first in E flat
has the rarity, in the later Brahms, of a poetic superscription: some
lines of a Scottish lullaby taken (as with 'Edward' of Op. 10) from
the German of Herder's folksong collection – 'Schlaf sanft, mein
Kind'. The folk-like tune, of masterly 'simplicity', made it an
instant success, and an abortive attempt to orchestrate it stressed
its intimate pianistic nature. The theme is subtly scored in an
inner part, requiring a fastidious attention to balance. Yet even
here Brahms amuses himself with some gentle brain-work. In
bars 13 and 14 he begins to rock the cradle in 3/4 time instead of
6/8, introducing an imitation in the lower notes of the right hand;
and when the passage returns he restores the 6/8 lilt but makes a
strict canon out of the imitation – Ex. 27 overleaf.

With the deeper thoughts of the *più adagio* interlude the pianist
must 'forget his public entirely' and observe that it is sometimes the
lower right-hand notes and sometimes the upper that are to be
held through. Brahms took an increasing care over such details of
notation, and the following Intermezzo in B flat minor (no. 2) is

too full of instances to quote. Its opening is like a variation on a theme as yet unheard, with a melodic line more implied than revealed, an effect easily spoilt by the player who 'makes a tune' of the top part from the start. Again Brahms specified the notes to be held by 'double-stemming' them, and the experienced composer does not waste or conserve ink without reason. The point is that these shadowy arpeggios yield to the latent theme itself in the middle section, warmly harmonic and in the relative major of D flat. Perhaps 'middle section' is the wrong description, for Op. 117 no. 2 goes beyond the simpler ternary form of its companions, making a miniature sonata form with 'monothematic' first and second subjects. The free translation of the D flat theme into the tonic minor at the end (albeit with many promises of B flat major) has plenty of precedents in Mozart's minor-key returns; but the rich orchestral sonority over a pedal-note is more reminiscent of the sombre moods of Brahms's First Symphony (e.g. the first movement from bar 273 onwards).

The C sharp minor Intermezzo, Op. 117 no. 3, begins even more darkly. A bleak unison theme, with adjacent notes slurred in pairs, looks towards the first of Brahms's Four Serious Songs, a still later work. His pessimistic attitude to death was the reverse of Mozart's 'true goal of our existence' and the feeling of profound regret can be detected in many of his non-vocal works. But whereas the song in question, 'Denn es gehet dem Menschen wie dem Vieh', later rises in vehement protest, the Intermezzo finds consolation in two of the most beautifully textured pages in the whole of Brahms's piano music. Though the key is now A major it has, inevitably for him, its sad minor-key inflections (the F naturals and C naturals in Ex. 28):

Ex.28

## SIX PIANO-PIECES, OP. 118

The death of Elisabet von Herzogenberg in 1892 at the age of forty-five must have increased Brahms's pessimism. Her husband, himself a composer, continued to correspond with him: 'I have at last purchased your glorious *Klavierstücke* (Opp. 118 and 119) and ordered the entertaining fifty-one finger-torturers (the Uebungen). I am looking forward to hearing Frau Schumann play my favourites.' But Clara was now well into her seventies, her powers failing, her hearing afflicted, and she was to die, a year before Brahms, in 1896. Her stamina had never been up to Brahms's severer pianistic demands but she could still take pleasure in the gentler of the Intermezzi, more of which had followed. Not all were as reflective as the three of Op. 117. Nos. 1 and 4 from Op. 118 seem to have inherited the manner of the former Capricci, a title that has now disappeared for good. The first, an Intermezzo in A minor, has a passionate character and a broad sweeping theme, only establishing its home-key towards the end. The opening emphasises the note B flat, giving a strong flavour of F major and leading the short first 'half' to a cadence in *its* dominant of C major. Cutting upwards across the descent of the theme are some typically widespread arpeggios that declare the name of Brahms from their very look. The 'open' effect of a rising third followed by a rising sixth, omitting one note of the traditional triad, may be dictated and varied for reasons of grammar and euphony, and the advice against sounding a stressed dissonance together with its resolution (except in the bass) was an age-old generalisation. But notice how Brahms preserves this third-sixth pattern at the end, where most composers would have touched the fifth of the chord somewhere on the way up (Ex. 29). The fingerprint is unmistakable and has perhaps a symbolic significance. Thirds and sixths Brahms loved; but transpose the quotation into F major and the intervals become FAF, the 'frei aber froh' motto that haunted him since his early days with Joachim.

Ex.29

The major ending here prepares naturally for the second Intermezzo, no. 2 in A major, and as nos. 4 and 5 have a similar relationship there seems more intention of a definite 'set' than previously.

No. 2 is outstandingly beautiful and technically within reach of a good amateur player. It contains quite a few contrapuntal devices, but they are now so assimilated that they are hardly noted as such, a tribute to the art that conceals art. The opening phrases sound warm-hearted and spontaneous whichever way one looks at them. They may be inverted (bars 34–6) or serve as a bass to another theme (bars 31–4), and throughout there is a sense of richness achieved largely with diatonic harmony. The 'trio' is in F sharp minor (compare Op. 76 no. 6) and in its progress the alert listener may discern augmentation, canon, and double counterpoint. A close canon is in fact concealed in the left-hand chords of the most rapt passage of all, a *pianissimo* turn to F sharp major. From the cadence of this middle section Brahms 'builds a bridge' back to the return of the opening, and in so doing proves a slender but vital thematic kinship. He does so without for one moment 'renouncing beauty and emotion' (as Schoenberg put it), and the beauty and emotion cannot be so readily analysed.

Two surprise titles are in store at this stage. Op. 118 no. 3 is a fiery Ballade in G minor, a name Brahms had not used in his piano music since the early Op. 10 set. It opens in a swaggering heroic manner, soon becoming quieter and clouded with Neapolitan harmonies, but with a fine climax to round off the first part. (The now familiar ternary form brings this back in full with the dramatic difference of a minor in place of a major-key ending.) A rhythmic pattern persists throughout, raising a performing problem similar to some encountered in the Handel Variations and serious enough to suggest a miscalculation on Brahms's part. In brief, the main notes of the theme – which one imagines should ring out with the brilliance of a trumpet – are so placed that the energetic chordal accompaniment usually obliterates them:

Ex.30

**Allegro energico**

What *should* sound in the rhythm

making a ragtime out of a challenging gesture. Brahms could scarcely have intended this, and it would have been revealing to have heard him play the piece himself. With sustaining wind and contrasting strings there would have been no such problem, and the actual notation does not permit ambiguity: in *piano*, with the accompaniment subdued, there is no problem either for a skilled player with an ear sensitive to the instrument's inevitable *diminuendo*. Such a moment comes in a far-away key during the middle section, a lullaby introduced through a magic modulation. Here the scrupulous composer picked out with extra quaver-tails the left-hand harmonic changes *not* to be blurred with the pedal.

A further Intermezzo (Op. 118 no. 4) is a strange F minor affair, at first absorbed with suppressed but agitated exchanges between the hands. In his book in the *Master Musicians* series Peter Latham aptly described it as 'rich in canons but somewhat dour'. An A flat departure – one cannot for ever talk of trios and middle sections – looks on paper like another purely intellectual exercise, with the left hand meticulously following and fitting in with every move of the right, but in practice it produces a warmly melodic effect. The return is climactic, stormy and formally free, but the final F major chord is given time to fade away quietly – in preparation for no. 5 in this key? This brings the other 'surprise' title, a Romanze – with a subject more comfortable than comforting and a melodic line intriguingly elusive, as anyone who tries to sing it will soon discover.

Where (as was asked of Op. 116 no. 6) is the tune – in the top line or in the richly doubled inner voices? In both apparently, since divorce is out of the question: the lines interchange with the lower one coming to the surface from time to time, but they are never heard separately. The form is again ternary, with an interlude carried through in continuous variations over a rocking bass *ostinato* (like Chopin's *Berceuse*): there is a curiously Sibelian flavour in the harmony at each fourth bar, a Lydian mixture of G sharps in the prevailing D major, but it will sound less exotic to those who have sung in the pedal-note fugue (in the same key) of the Brahms Requiem.

It was once rumoured that the last of these Op. 118 pieces, the profoundly tragic and in turn dramatic Intermezzo in E flat minor, was considered by Brahms as material for the slow movement of an unwritten further symphony. Yet to return to Richard Specht's first-hand memories of Brahms's playing in those last years, it would have been in his opinion a sacrilege to drag such a secret-laden piece 'out into the glaring light of the concert room'. Symphonies may still, however, hold their intimate secrets; and the intimacies of the greatest chamber music may be vouchsafed to a large audience that in any case consists of individuals. As an experiment, not necessarily for publication or even performance, a devoted student of Brahms might try out an orchestration of the E flat minor Intermezzo, beginning with a duet for clarinet and harp. The idea is not so outrageous, for Brahms's left-hand writing is decidedly harp-like (Ex. 31): and his late love for the clarinet resulted in a whole series of works written for Richard Mühlfeld, whom he had first heard in the Meiningen Orchestra in 1891, two years before the completion and publication of the Op. 118 *Klavierstücke*.

Ex.31

**Andante, largo e mesto**

Pianists could learn much from such an experiment and even from the thought of it, though opinions would differ when overlapping thirds are added to the continuation of the forlorn opening theme: strings or woodwind, but surely a preference for interlacing pairs of wind instruments? Whatever is decided, the remainder of the orchestra, spectators so far, will join in progressively from the entry of the new theme in G flat – until the great climax suddenly collapses, dispersing and silencing most of them again.

### FOUR PIANO-PIECES, OP. 119

This final set, probably overlapping the previous one in composition (both were published in 1893), makes an unusual unity – if unity was in fact intended – out of increasing animation. The Intermezzo in B minor, Op. 119 no. 1, 'so sadly sweet' to Clara Schumann 'in spite of all its dissonances', is an *adagio* in mood as well as tempo; and the Rhapsody in E flat seems a complete anachronism in its evocation of an energetic, much younger Brahms. Yet it is stylistically prepared by two intervening Intermezzi, through stages of agitation (no. 2) and lively humour (no. 3). In the experimenting frame of mind encouraged just now by Op. 118 no. 6 the open volume of the complete piano music suggests a further experiment. That E flat minor Intermezzo had closed with a conventional arpeggio unfolding upwards to the tonic. Heard in juxtaposition the opening of Op. 119 no. 1 makes an exquisite enharmonic modulation, translating the next (but unheard) arpeggio-note, G flat, into an F sharp folding downwards in thirds. This is all wishful thinking, of course, since there can hardly have been any intentional link between the end of one set and the start of another: but some of the E flat minor's mood of tragic pathos could appear to have rubbed off on to the B minor, and the counterpoint in thirds (bars 5 and 7) adds to the inheritance, conscious or not.

Falling thirds, heard from the outset of Op. 119 no. 1, had long been a Brahmsian characteristic – from the *andante* of the F minor Sonata to the opening of the Fourth Symphony and beyond. (In the Four Serious Songs they express the bitterness of death but are transformed into rising major sixths at mention of its consolation, a simple technical device that warms both mind and heart when used with such artistry.) In the B minor Intermezzo they are suspended, thus producing Clara's 'dissonances', and part of the fascination of the piece (charm is too frivolous a word) lies in the new harmonic complexes set up by the resolution, like a Chinese puzzle. Other expected traits are still present and, as with Op. 118 no. 2, now perfectly integrated: in bar 4 the left hand begins answering the right in canon, and the middle D major section inevitably brings a closing-up into cross-rhythms as its theme aspires to its climax. The falling thirds are touched in with passing-notes on their return, but the extra notes literally 'pass', as in Baroque practice, and as Brahms carefully indicates. The real release is left for the penultimate bar, a resolution in perfect accordance with Classical principles: only then is the puzzle 'solved'.

The second Intermezzo (E minor) is extremely 'monothematic' in the way it is drawn back repeatedly to its first phrase in various guises and variations. Their attempts to establish new keys (A minor, F minor) are short-lived, giving an air of restlessness that is summed up in the marking 'un poco agitato'. It remains for the self-contained E major section to develop an idea continuously, though the idea itself is yet another variant of the opening, transforming the melodic contours into a graceful and leisurely waltz (Ex. 32 overleaf). A brief memory of this forms the coda.

No. 3 in C major, though called Intermezzo, has the character of a miniature scherzo. Only the more turbulent connections with the term Capriccio can have prevented Brahms using it here. It is wholly witty, playful and compact, all over within a couple of

minutes, and the wit does not exclude a lyrical tenderness that emerges on the last page. There is even a rare touch of self-parody in its humorous treatment of the cross-rhythms that Brahms had elsewhere employed so seriously. They are inherent in the subject, which is heard and developed mostly as an inner part (another parody?), and their initial ambiguity adds to the wittiness.

After such lightness of manner the final Rhapsody, Op. 119 no. 4, was bound to appear uncompromisingly solid. Yet to have referred to it just now as an 'anachronism' is perhaps wrong, since this last set of pieces could also be regarded as a deliberate summing-up of Brahms's complex and sometimes contradictory nature. The three Intermezzi of Op. 119 are complementary: the B minor's deep meditation, the E minor's brief and restless toying with variation techniques giving way to the pure song of the major key, and the C major's wit and humour. The Rhapsody completes the picture by reverting to the grand manner. Its block chords recall the equally solid opening of the early C major Sonata, and the sombre triplets of its C minor episodes could be interchanged with those near the start of the F minor Sonata by the simple expedient of a change of bar line and a Brahmsian hemiola! It could never suffer, like some of the 'secret-laden' Intermezzi, by being brought into the glaring light. Unlike the rest of these late pieces it seems designed for public performance. This one *could* have been successfully orchestrated by Brahms and one almost wishes he had done it (in the personal opinion of a player who has often longed for a dramatic entry of brass and timpani on the accented chords in bars 4 to 6 and other places). The form, needless to say, is far from rhapsodic in the Lisztian sense, though from a Brahmsian viewpoint more so than in either of the Op. 79 pair. It may be described as an arch, with the one lyrical and gracefully scored A flat theme at the centre, led up to and away from by the C minor-major triplets. A rousing chordal theme and its accessories dominate the beginning and the end, with a lengthy, largely subdued and very 'orchestral' preparation for the latter, amounting to a kind of development section. Yet the three full statements of the theme also leave one with the impression of a rondo. Each takes a different harmonic twist at its climax, the final statement landing resolutely in the tonic minor, in which key the Rhapsody surprisingly ends. Schubert had made a similar move at the end of his Impromptu in the same key. The effect in performance is convincing, with no loss of a feeling of triumph, perhaps because E flat minor had (in both cases) loomed large earlier on. The coda gave Brahms a chance of rounding up his favourite iambic dotted rhythm, which had not hitherto appeared, thus enhancing the 'self-portrait' impression of the series.

## Retrospect

The title 'Rückblick' (retrospect) was applied by the twenty-year-old Brahms to the 'extra' fourth movement of his F minor Sonata, Op. 5, which recalls the idyllic second movement theme in regretful nostalgic tones. A longing to 'look back' characterised his life's work. It was somehow fitting that his very last composition should have been the Eleven Chorale Preludes for organ, ending with 'O Welt, ich muss dich lassen'. His love of Bach was paramount, his indebtedness to Beethoven obvious, and one of his most treasured possessions was the manuscript of Mozart's great G minor Symphony. These influences remained vital, and in spite of some contrary prophecies Brahms's music in general has proved its own vitality. On the subject of his supposed conservatism Schoenberg was quoted earlier, and he must be again:

It is important to realise that at a time when all believed in 'expression', Brahms, without renouncing beauty and emotion, proved to be a progressive in a field which had not been cultivated for half a century. He would have been a pioneer if he had simply returned to Mozart.

Then followed Schoenberg's remark about 'not living on inherited fortune'. The present-day standing of Brahms's symphonies and concertos is real proof of this, and it is hoped that a definite relation has been established between their achievement and the changing 'phases' of his piano music. Progress in art is not to be measured by mere innovation, and though Schoenberg himself became one of the most famous of musical innovators he admitted that he arrived at his new 'method' (of twelve-note composition) through 'necessity'. The need for discipline in a world of growing harmonic indulgence and complexity was made clear to him, and the parallel with Brahms's earlier Romantic background and *his* needs is not so far-fetched. It may be amusing to note that in 1893, the year of Brahms's last piano-pieces, Debussy was composing his *Prélude à l'après-midi d'un faune*. But Brahms's steadfast allegiance to the past can no longer blind one to his originality, for he was also an innovator in that his style is unmistakable. One often hears it said of other composers' works that they have Brahmsian sixths and thirds, Brahmsian textures or cross-rhythms.

Not all Brahms's piano music is regularly played today. Of the early sonatas the F minor seems the only firm repertory work, and the Handel and Paganini variations easily outstrip the other variation-sets in popularity. The later pieces are seldom played as complete groups, and a handful of favourites tends to predominate. This is not to dispute the rewards that await the performer and listener in some of the less-played ones, for Brahms was too much of a craftsman and far too self-critical to pass anything shoddy or second-best. Yet his craftsmanship and integrity, with his desire for demonstrable logic at all costs, led at times to duplication of treatment and standardisation of emotion. A complete Brahms 'cycle', for example, could hardly be as rewardingly varied as the whole series of Beethoven's piano sonatas. In reviewing all Brahms's piano works I have occasionally felt embarrassment at the recurrence of such descriptive words as 'hemiola', 'ternary form' and 'double counterpoint'; or even more subjective ones like 'passionate' and 'reflective'. On the other hand no one presumably is likely to sort out all Brahms's pieces of a kind and to play them at one sitting, hough something has been written about every one of them here in fulfilment of the book's purpose as a guide. The most satisfyingly varied Brahms recital will probably choose from each of his 'three phases' – which takes us back to our starting-point.

# Index of Works Discussed